THINKING IN THREES

THE POWER OF THREE IN WRITING

Brian Backman

Routledge
Taylor & Francis Group

NEW YORK AND LONDON

First published in 2005 by Prufrock.Press Inc.

Published in 2021 by Routledge
605 Third Avenue, New York, NY 10017
2 Park Square, Milton Park, Abingdon, Oxon OX14 4RN

Routledge is an imprint of the Taylor & Francis Group, an informa business.

ISBN: 9781032141572 (hbk)
ISBN: 9781877673672 (pbk)

DOI: 10.4324/9781003239048

For Joy, Sam, and Max — my most important trio

TABLE OF CONTENTS

A NOTE FOR TEACHERS

"There are three rules for writing the novel.
Unfortunately, no one knows what they are."
—W. Somerset Maugham

The rules for writing a novel may be a mystery, but when it comes to the essay, there is no shortage of books offering rules and advice. So what is it that makes this book different? In a nutshell, the difference is that it gives students writing strategies organized in easy-to-remember groups of three. It supplies students with immediately applicable tools to improve their writing, whether they are writing a timed essay in 25 minutes or a polished essay over the course of two weeks. To sum it up, this is a book about the power of *threes*.

Here's a sneak preview of some of the "rules of three" explained in this book:

- Three steps for brainstorming
- Three "p's" of a thesis statement
- Three parts of an essay
- Three paragraphs in the body of an essay
- Three ways to connect paragraphs and sentences
- Three types of evidence to support topic sentences
- Three qualities of a good example
- Three things to include in a quotation
- Three ways to hook the reader in an introduction
- Three ways to write fluent sentences
- Three ways to write successful conclusions
- Three phases of completing a timed writing assignment.

In addition, sprinkled throughout the book are "Three Point Shot" activities, which help students see the power of three in action in the words, phrases, and sentences of great writers.

There are essentially *three* ways you can use the book:

APPROACH 1: START AT THE BEGINNING AND PROCEED IN ORDER TO THE END.
The book is organized so that students will gain strategies that will build on each other logically from beginning to end. You can assign an essay at any time or wait until students have completed all of the exercises in the book. You can also use the sample essays at the end of the book to illustrate concepts. The first essay, "A Miracle Cure-All" (page 93), is the simplest. The second, "Why Memorize and Recite?" (page 95), is suitable for more advanced students. Also included is an example of a timed essay, "Failure: Springboard to Success" (page 88).

**APPROACH 2: SELECT A PARTICULAR SECTION BASED ON YOUR STUDENTS'
IMMEDIATE NEED.** Because each section is self-contained, you can sample a particular section

without worrying about any of the preceding sections. For example, if you want your students to work on introductory "hooks" before you teach the thesis, you don't have to worry about being out of sequence.

APPROACH 3: ASSIGN SECTIONS INDIVIDUALLY BASED ON INDIVIDUAL STUDENT WEAKNESSES. After evaluating a group of essays, you might assign different sections of this book to different students, based on individual or group needs. For example, some students might need help on their introductions, while others might need help on sentence fluency.

Whichever approach you choose, the goal of this book is the same: to give students specific strategies that they can apply immediately to improve their writing.

Brian Backman

THE POWER OF THREE

THREE, THREE, THREE

Lights! Camera! Action!	*All good things come in threes.* Norwegian proverb	*Ready! Aim! Fire!*

There is something special, maybe even magical, about the number *three*. It's everywhere. It's omnipresent. It's *ubiquitous* (a good word to learn!).

- Speech coaches explain to their students that the audience more readily remembers something if it is repeated *three* times.

- Military instructors teach their soldiers to limit their focus to *three* tasks or goals.

- Comedians use a *three*-part formula for jokes. First, they set up the situation; then they continue the theme; and finally they twist the theme around, delivering the punch line.

- Memorable historical speeches often include *three*-part lines:

    - *Friends, Romans, countrymen…*(William Shakespeare)

    - *Government of the people, by the people, for the people.* (Abraham Lincoln)

    - *Free at last! Free at last! Thank God Almighty, we are free at last!* (Martin Luther King)

- Good teachers know that people learn better in *threes:* reading about something, writing about it, and speaking about it.

- Advertisers create memorable slogans using *three*-beat lines: "The few, the proud, the Marines," or simple *three*-word catch phrases: "Just do it."

- Sales trainers teach their salespeople to give the buyer *three* reasons to buy the product, *three* benefits of the product, *three* testimonials from satisfied customers, and finally, *three* choices on how to purchase the product.

    As you can see, thinking in threes is not hard to do because *threes* are all around us.

DO IT NOW   Think of at least three other examples of the use of *three* in life.

1. _____

   _____

2. _____

   _____

3. _____

   _____

TRIPLETS

The number *three* is powerful, magical, and memorable. See if you can complete these famous triplets.

1. Breakfast, lunch, and _____.

2. _____, paper, and scissors.

3. Knife, _____, and spoon.

4. Lions, tigers, and _____.

5. Hear no evil, _____, speak no evil.

6. _____, willing, and able.

7. Lock, _____, and barrel.

8. Life, liberty, and the pursuit of _____.

9. _____, legislative, and executive.

10. Snap, _____, pop.

11. Yesterday, today, and _____.

12. _____, vegetable, or mineral.

13. Hop, _____, and jump.

14. Red, yellow, _____.

15. _____, place, show.

DO IT NOW Now, see if you can think of some common triplets of your own:

1. _____.

2. _____.

3. _____.

4. _____.

5. _____.

6. _____.

THREE THINGS TO SAY

The number *three* has a great deal of power when it comes to writing. Learning how to harness the power of three will make each phase of the writing process simpler, more efficient, and more logical.

Here is the most basic rule of all about the power of three:

WHEN FACED WITH A WRITING TASK, THINK OF THREE THINGS YOU CAN SAY ABOUT YOUR TOPIC.

It may sound simple, but the results can be profound. Taking any writing task and breaking it into three parts will help you write better. It will also help you with the important task of pleasing your reader. (People *like* reading sets of three.)

Let's look at how it works. Suppose you receive this question on an essay history test:

How did World War II change the course of history?

Following the basic rule about the power of three, you would first reword the question (either in your head or on paper) so that it includes *three*. You might come up with something like this:

What are three ways in which World War II changed the course of history?

or

What are three key battles in World War II that changed the course of history?

Rewording the question to include *three* will help you remember to find three things to say about your topic.

DO IT NOW Put the basic rule of three into action by rewriting the questions below so that they include *three*.

1. What makes you unique?

2. What things about your hometown would you mention to promote tourism?

3. What exactly do you like about your favorite movie or television program?

4. What things should a person *not* do during a speech?

5. Why should children have pets?

6. How can you be kind on a daily basis?

7. What qualities make an effective leader?

8. What is your favorite book? What do you like about it?

JUST THREE WORDS

The three most lethal words in a traveler's lexicon are *you never know*. —Gerald Nachman

The three most beautiful words in the English language: *We the people*. —Benazir Bhutto

My three least favorite words are *I don't care*. —James Caan

In three words I can sum up everything I've learned about life: *It goes on*. —Robert Frost

These are the three most important words to remember when you're
being deposed: *I don't know*. —William Bernhardt

The three most important words in the English language: *Wait a minute*. —Sam Raburn

DO IT NOW Shakespeare wrote, "Brevity is the soul of wit." The quotations above
show the power of concise language, featuring *three* in some way.

Write *three* "Three most...." or "Three least...." sentences of your own, expressing *your* opinions.

1. _____

    _____

2. _____

    _____

3. _____

    _____

BRAINSTORMING

THREE STEPS FOR BRAINSTORMING

When walking through the woods one day, Goldilocks came upon a house. The door was open, so she walked in and found three bowls of porridge. She tried the first bowl, but it was too hot. She tried the second bowl, but it was too cold. Then she tried the third bowl, and it was just right.

After her meal, Goldilocks was feeling tired, so she decided to look for a place to rest. She looked around and couldn't find a bed on the first floor, so she climbed the steps and found a bedroom. She hopped in the bed and exclaimed, "This bed is too hard." She wandered down the hall and went into another bedroom. She jumped onto the bed and said, "This bed is too soft." Very tired, she walked down the hall into a third bedroom. As she entered the room, she yelled out in surprise as she saw three small pink pigs in the corner of the room. "Hey, you guys," she said. "Don't you know you're in the wrong fairy tale?"

"No, we're not," answered one of the pigs. "The three bears live on the first floor, we live on the second floor, and the three billy goats gruff live on the third floor."

"That's the silliest thing I've ever heard," answered Goldilocks.

"What's so silly?" responded the pig, "Don't you know this is a three-story house?"

We begin learning about the power of three in childhood. Many of the characters from children's stories come in threes, and so do some other elements: three bowls, three beds, three wishes, etc.

Even though you may have outgrown fairy tales, the power of three can still help you when you write your own stories and essays. Like Goldilocks, good writers are in search of that "just right" balance. Using the power of three as a planning tool will help you avoid the danger of saying too much and avoid the peril of saying too little.

A writing assignment typically begins with an open-ended question. The best way to begin is by *brainstorming*. When you brainstorm, follow these three steps:

STATE THE QUESTION. Whether you are brainstorming alone or in a group, make sure you clearly state the question you are trying to answer before you begin. Write it down, so you can see it as you think. (If you are given a topic that is *not* a question, turn it into a question before you begin brainstorming. For example, if your topic is "school rules," you might write this question: What are three school rules our school should eliminate?)

GENERATE MANY IDEAS. Photographers know that less than one picture in ten is worth saving. It's the same with ideas. Always go for *quantity* when brainstorming, and resist the temptation to stop after you have written down a few ideas. Instead, keep going. If possible, springboard off the ideas of others.

SUSPEND YOUR CRITICISM. Brainstorming is a creative exercise, not a critical exercise. Try to temporarily suspend the critical, judgmental side of your brain—the left hemisphere. Instead, use the creative side of your brain, the right hemisphere, to generate as many ideas as you can. Write down everything. No idea is too silly or strange. Don't comment on the ideas; just write them down as they come.

After completing a brainstorming session, look back over your list for the best ideas. Select your *three* best, and write them down.

BRAINSTORMING IN ACTION
AN EXAMPLE

State the question.
Generate many ideas.
Suspend your criticism.

Imagine that Mary is writing on the topic of "effects of television on young people." First, she turns the topic into a question that includes *three*. She decides on, "What are three effects of television on young people?" As Mary brainstorms ideas, she decides to look at both sides of the question and think of both the positive and the negative effects of television.

Question: What are three effects of television on young people?

POSITIVE EFFECTS	NEGATIVE EFFECTS
educational TV	waste of time
fitness TV	infomercials
keeps you entertained	keeps you inside
gets news to you fast	distracting
teaches language	makes you lazy
opportunity to see different international events	stations dictate what you see
	inappropriate programs for children
keeps you up-to-date	causes binge eating
diversity of programs	commercials
unlimited content	addictive
children's programs	stressful
relaxing	false advertising
cultural variety	hurts your eyes
gives you something to do if you're bored	promotes violence

After brainstorming a number of ideas, Mary looks over her list to select the three ideas that are the strongest, and she decides which side she is going to argue. She decides her final question will be, "What are three positive effects of television on young people?" Her final three reasons, taken from her brainstormed list, are:

1. Television helps you learn.
2. Television gives you information from all over the world.
3. Television allows you to relax.

This may not look like much, but in reality it is the foundation of her essay. Mary now has a main point—that television has a positive effect on young people. She also has a working outline with reasons that support her main point. She can begin her essay knowing that she has just the right balance. Like a perfectly formed triangle, Mary's three solid points will form the foundation of a well-written essay.

BRAINSTORMING PRACTICE

Brainstorm many ideas.
Then pick your three best.

Select one of the questions below and, on a separate page, brainstorm possible answers. Try for at least 20 different possible answers. As you work, remember the three rules for brainstorming:

State the question.
Generate many ideas.
Suspend your criticism.

1. What are the things about you that make you unique?

2. What are some things about your hometown that you might mention to promote tourism?

3. What are some things that you like about your favorite movie or television program?

4. Who do you think is the most influential person in history?

5. Who do you think is the most influential person living today?

6. What are things a person should *not* do during a speech?

7. What are the reasons that children should/should not have pets?

8. What are some ways to be kind on a daily basis?

9. What are the qualities that make an effective leader?

10. What is your favorite book? What are the reasons everyone should read it?

When you have finished brainstorming, circle your three best ideas.

ADVICE IN THREES

The list in the box, below, is the result of a brainstorm on the following question:

What are some examples of three-word pieces of advice?

Notice that each three-word piece of advice begins with a verb. Verbs are an important part of good writing. They enliven your writing with movement, action, and energy.

DO IT NOW The verbs are missing in the three-word pieces of advice below. See if you can fill in the blanks.

1. _____ on wood.
2. _____ and learn.
3. _____ the piper.
4. _____ my lips.
5. _____ a leg.
6. _____ my mind.
7. _____ the plunge.
8. _____ the line.
9. _____ my heart.
10. _____ the roof.

ACT YOUR AGE.
BITE THE BULLET.
BUTTON YOUR LIP.
COOL YOUR HEELS.
CUT IT SHORT.
DO OR DIE.
GO ALL OUT.
GRIND IT OUT.
HOLD YOUR HORSES.
HOLD THE FORT.

Now, add to this list of brief and pithy advice. Think of ten more three-word phrases that you have heard, or create your own.

1. _____   6. _____
2. _____   7. _____
3. _____   8. _____
4. _____   9. _____
5. _____   10. _____

WRITING A THESIS

THE THREE "P'S"
OF A THESIS STATEMENT

> *A doctor is sitting next to a complete stranger on a flight to New York City. He sees that the stranger is reading through some official looking documents. "You must be a lawyer," the doctor says to the stranger.*
>
> *"Yes, I am," replies the stranger.*
> *"So how much do you charge per hour?" asks the doctor.*
> *"I don't charge by the hour. I charge $500 for every three questions," answers the lawyer.*
> *The doctor replies, "Wow! Isn't that a lot of money for just three questions?"*
> *The lawyer answers, "Not really...so what's your third question?"*

An anecdote like the one above doesn't work if you give away the punch line. An essay, however, is a bit different. Your reader doesn't want to have to guess where you're going and expects a "road map" to see the route. Therefore, you need to give the reader a sneak preview of what is coming up on the road ahead. We call this sneak preview the *thesis* of your essay. A thesis is simply a one-sentence statement of your essay's main points.

A clearly written thesis keeps you on track by reminding you of your route, your direction, and your destination. And that brings us to an important "rule of three":

A GOOD THESIS STATEMENT INCLUDES THREE "P'S."
IT IS A THREE-PRONGED PARALLEL PREVIEW OF YOUR ESSAY.

Here's an example:

> *Television has a positive effect because it helps you learn;*
> *it gives you information from all over the world; and it allows you to relax.*

- The three **p**rongs are the three ways it has a positive effect. (It helps you learn; it gives you information from all over the world; it allows you to relax.)
- The three prongs are written in **p**arallel form, which means they have the same grammatical structure. (In this case, each prong begins with "it.")
- The thesis gives us a **p**review of what the essay will be about. (It's going to be about the positive effects of television.)

PARALLELISM IN ACTION
EXAMPLES

Items are in parallel form when they have the same grammatical structure. For example, if each item in a list is an "ing" word, the items are written in parallel form. If a series of sentences each begins with the words, "There are…," the sentences are written in parallel form.

It is a good idea to put any kind of list or series in parallel form. It is especially important when writing a thesis.

WHY PARALLEL? The following illustration may help you see the logic behind putting items in parallel form. Imagine you are putting together a poster that announces some upcoming homecoming activities. Which of the two posters below states the information most clearly?

HOMECOMING 2005	HOMECOMING 2005
Decorate halls.	*Decorate halls.*
Float building.	*Build floats.*
The football game.	*Attend football game.*

You probably picked the poster on the right. Because all three items are stated in parallel form, they are easier to understand. Each item starts with a verb that describes one of the homecoming activities.

Notice the differences in the non-parallel and the parallel thesis statements below:

NON-PARALLEL THESIS: Anacortes, Washington, is a great place to live because of its beautiful forest lands, its small town feel, and it has a low crime rate.

PARALLEL THESIS: Anacortes, Washington, is a great place to live because of its beautiful forest lands, its small town feel, and its low crime rate.

NON-PARALLEL THESIS: The most important qualities of a good friend are a sense of humor, being kind, and someone I can depend on.

PARALLEL THESIS: The most important qualities of a good friend are a sense of humor, kindness, and dependability.

Packing all three ideas into a single sentence can be a challenge, but using parallelism will make the task easier, and it will make your thesis clear, logical, and concise.

PRACTICE WITH PARALLEL FORM

A good thesis statement includes three "p's."
It is a three-pronged parallel preview of your essay.

DO IT NOW | Read the thesis sentences below. Determine which sentences are correct and which need to be revised so that they are written in parallel form. Write "Correct" next to the correct thesis sentences. Revise the incorrect sentences.

1. Sports benefit your overall health because they relieve stress in your muscles, they work your cardiovascular system, and your brain needs oxygen.

2. Computers are helpful because they are a way to communicate, a way to get work done faster, and a way to entertain yourself.

3. William Shakespeare is influential because of his poetry, his plays, and because he coined so many new words.

4. Every student should complete high school because high school graduates earn more, finding better jobs, and they have more choices.

5. Every child should have a pet because pets provide companionship, teach compassion, and encourage responsibility.

PRACTICE WRITING A THESIS

A good thesis statement includes three "p's."
It is a three-pronged parallel preview of your essay.

DO IT NOW In the box are brainstormed results based on an open-ended question. Select the three qualities you think answer the question best, and then write a thesis. Make sure that your thesis includes three points stated in parallel form.

Question: What are three qualities of an effective leader?

integrity	hard work	honesty
good looking	taller than six feet	rides a horse
bravery	just and fair	ability to speak and motivate
no visible tan lines	powerful voice	relates well to young people
cool shades	cowboy boots	skill and ability
personable	not prejudiced	a visionary
smart	logical	strong-minded
careful	determined	quick-witted
strict	successful	calm
charismatic	good at job	able to keep control
not simple-minded	good common sense	tactical
trustworthy	listens	commands well
reliable	loud	talkative
multitasks	headstrong	gives his or her all
has connections	respected	motivated
ready for anything	keeps pace	cracks down
has pride	not faltering	knows when to react
realizes flaws	knows the issues	knows how to respond
has a plan	not rash	good communication skills

YOUR THESIS:

_____

_____

_____

_____

PUTTING IT TOGETHER

A good thesis statement includes three "p's."
It is a three-pronged parallel preview of your essay.

DO IT NOW Look at ideas you have already generated in a brainstorm, or start over with a new question and brainstorm ideas. Then write a thesis that incorporates your three best ideas. Make sure that your thesis is a three-pronged, parallel preview and that it is grammatically correct.

EXAMPLE:

Question: Should high school students work during the school year?
Top three brainstormed answers:

- High school students should not work during the school year because a job interrupts their studying schedule.
- It interrupts their social schedule.
- It interrupts their sleeping schedule.

Thesis: High school students should not work during the school year because a job interrupts their study schedule, their social schedule, and their sleep schedule.

Your question:

Your top three brainstormed answers:

Your thesis:

THREE IMPORTANT THINGS

Human beings respond well to the number *three*. We like to hear *three* reasons for doing something. We like fairy tales that involve *three* wishes. We like jokes with *three* parts leading to a punch line.

The quotations below use *three* to organize sentences that are clear, rhythmic, and insightful:

Folks are serious about three things—their religion,
their family, and most of all, their money. —Bert Lance

"I've learned that you can tell a lot about a person by the way he/she handles these three things:
a rainy day, lost luggage, and tangled Christmas tree lights. —Maya Angelou

"There are three things you cannot hide: coughing, poverty, and love." —Yiddish proverb

"There are three things which if a man does not know he cannot live long in the world:
what is too much for him, what is too little for him, and what is just right for him." —Swahili proverb

"The three best things about teaching are June, July, and August." —Bill Kane

I learned three important things in college—to use a library, to memorize quickly and visually,
to drop asleep at any time given a horizontal surface and fifteen minutes. —Agnes De Mille

DO IT NOW Here's your chance to say three things about topics that concern you. Create three different quotable quotes of your own. Each must contain the words "three things." If you have trouble coming up with ideas, the following sentence starters might help:

The three most important things about _____ are...
The three keys to life are...
Success in _____ requires three things:

1. _____

_____

2. _____

_____

3. _____

_____

Organizing an Essay

THREE PARAGRAPHS
IN THE BODY OF AN ESSAY

As a husband is leaving his home to go to work one morning, his wife says, "I'll bet you don't know what day it is today."

"Of course I do," the husband answers indignantly.

At 10:00 a.m., there is a knock at the door and the wife finds a dozen long-stemmed red roses.

At 1:00 p.m., a huge box of her favorite chocolates arrives at the door.

At 5:00 p.m., a dress designed by the most exclusive boutique in town is delivered.

The wife, anxious for her husband to arrive home, meets him as he walks up to the front door and says, "Wow, the three gifts you sent were great! First the roses, then the chocolate, and finally the dress! I've never had a better Groundhog Day in my life!!"

Before the husband realizes it really isn't his anniversary, he comes up with *three* appropriate gifts; somehow three separate gifts seem just right for such an important occasion. Similarly, coming up with *three* ideas that relate directly to your main point will help you lay the foundation for a solid essay.

AN ESSAY HAS THREE PARTS. Every essay needs three parts: a beginning, a middle, and an end. The beginning we call the *introduction*, the middle we call the *body*, and the end we call the *conclusion*. The first paragraph of your essay, the introduction, will contain the thesis.

THE BODY OF AN ESSAY HAS THREE PARTS. The body of a typical essay has three paragraphs. The three paragraphs support the thesis with clear reasons, clear evidence, and clear explanation. If you have written a good thesis—a three-pronged parallel preview—you will have created the organization of your paper. Each of the three points from your thesis sentence will magically become one of your topic sentences.

Here's an example:

Thesis: *Sports benefit your overall health because they relieve stress in your muscles; they work your cardiovascular system; and they provide oxygen to your brain.*

Topic Sentence 1: Sports benefit your overall health by relieving stress in your muscles.

Topic Sentence 2: Sports also benefit your overall health by working your cardiovascular system.

Topic Sentence 3: Finally, sports benefit your overall health by providing oxygen to your brain.

THREE WAYS
TO CONNECT PARAGRAPHS AND SENTENCES

Connecting paragraphs and sentences helps your reader follow your train of thought smoothly from beginning to end. There are three different techniques that will help you link each of your paragraphs and sentences.

THREE WAYS TO CONNECT SENTENCES AND PARAGRAPHS ARE WITH TRANSITION WORDS, PRONOUNS, AND REPETITION.

1. TRANSITION WORDS. Transition words are like traffic signals that you place in your writing to help guide your reader. They help the reader follow the progress of your writing and not get lost along the way. Here are just a few examples of transition words and phrases:

> for example • however • in addition • then • first
> second • in conclusion • because • and • but • after
> before • consequently • therefore • although • thus

Notice how the sentences below progress very differently, depending on the transition words used:

John loves sports; <u>for example</u>, he has a basketball hoop in his driveway,
an Olympic-sized swimming pool in his backyard, and a horseshoe pit in his front yard.

John loves sports, <u>but</u> he hates to bowl.

John loves sports <u>because</u> his mother and father have always encouraged him
and have never forced him to participate.

In the first sentence the transition "for example" lets the reader know that the general statement will be followed with specifics. In the second sentence the transition word "but" lets the reader know that a contrast is coming. And finally, in the third sentence the transition word "because" lets the reader know that the writer is going to give a reason.

2. REPETITION. When you repeat a word, you create a link from one sentence to another or from one paragraph to another. This link helps your reader stay on track. (Watch out for too much repetition, however. If you have used the same word five or more times in a single paragraph, you should think about using a synonym. Another option is to use a pronoun.)

Notice how Winston Churchill uses repetition in the following passage to drive his point home:

Never give in—never, never, never, never, in nothing great or small, large or petty, never give in except to convictions of honor and good sense. Never yield to force; never yield to the apparently overwhelming might of the enemy.

3. PRONOUNS. Pronouns were invented to help you save space and to save your reader from reading the same word over and over again. But pronouns also serve to link your paragraphs and sentences. Notice the difference between the two passages below:

WITHOUT PRONOUNS:

Tiger Woods won the U.S. Open in the year 2000 by an unprecedented 15 strokes. Tiger Woods led wire to wire, shooting 65-69-71-67 in the four rounds of the tournament. Throughout the entire tournament, Tiger Woods did not three-putt a single time.

WITH PRONOUNS:

Tiger Woods won the U.S. Open in the year 2000 by an unprecedented 15 strokes. He led wire to wire, shooting 65-69-71-67 in the four rounds of the tournament. Throughout the entire tournament, he did not three-putt a single time.

THREES IN ACTION

*Three ways to connect sentences and paragraphs
are to use transition words, pronouns, and repetition.*

DO IT NOW Read the sample essay below. Notice how it is organized. Fill out this simple organization chart below. Then underline all of the transition words, pronouns, and examples of repetition.

Thesis Statement: _____

_____

_____

Topic Sentence Paragraph #1: _____

_____

_____

Topic Sentence Paragraph #2: _____

_____

_____

Topic Sentence Paragraph #3: _____

_____

_____

THE PERFECT COMBINATION

He was named the man of the millennium by *Life* magazine; he was *Parade Magazine*'s top American innovator; and he made it into the top 40 in a book that ranked the most influential persons of all time. Although he died in 1931, no one has come close to the creative energy and productivity of inventor Thomas Edison. His genius was the perfect combination of innovative thinking, hard work, and a positive attitude.

No one before or after Edison has demonstrated such a capacity for innovative thinking. Edison generated an amazing quantity of new ideas and transformed those ideas into practical inventions that changed the lives of every man, woman, and child in America. He held over one thousand patents. The light bulb, phonograph, motion picture camera, telegraph, telephone, and typewriter are just a few of the innovations he either developed or improved (Hart 223). Not only were his ideas numerous, they were also practical. Edison's innovative thinking laid the

CONTINUED

foundation for the modern research laboratory. His Menlo Park laboratory was the prototype for modern companies such as General Electric that bring teams of people together to research, test, and manufacture the latest technology (Maxwell 90). Certainly he did not do everything alone; instead, his creative energy allowed him to work with and motivate others to produce and implement his ideas.

In addition to his creative genius, Edison also had a legendary capacity for hard work. Even though it took over ten thousand tries to find the correct materials for the incandescent light bulb, he did not give up until he found the answer. Many inventors would be fulfilled after filing a patent for just one invention, but Edison drove himself tirelessly to create, test, and improve his inventions. According to Edison biographer Neil Baldwin, "He was proud of the fact that certain times of the year he was away from home for one hundred nights in a row working in the lab" (Lamb 144). For Edison there was no retirement; only his death, in 1931 at age 84, put an end to his work.

Even though the combination of creativity and tireless drive made Edison a success, perhaps his more noteworthy trait was his positive attitude. Although he had only four months of formal education and was labeled "retarded" by one of his school teachers, Edison pursued his own education and achieved so much that today his name is synonymous with genius (Hart 222). Later in life he suffered from deafness, but he did not let this obstacle stop him. Instead, he went on to fill countless homes with music through the invention of the phonograph. When his laboratory burned down in 1914, he immediately rebuilt it and continued to work for another seventeen years. There was no "quit" in the man who said, "If we did all the things we were capable of doing, we would literally astound ourselves" (Maxwell 89).

Thomas Alva Edison's achievements were clearly astounding. His innovative thinking, his hard work, and his positive attitude allowed him to reach the apex of human potential. In Edison, the three chords of inspiration, perspiration, and attitude combined to create a symphony of achievements that should be a reminder to each of us that the only limits that exist in this world are the limits that we create in our own minds.

WORKS CITED

Baldwin, Neil. "Thomas Edison." *Booknotes Life Stories.* Ed. Brian Lamb. New York: Times Books, 1999.

Hart, Michael H. *The 100: A Ranking of the Most Influential Persons in History.* New York: Citadel Press, 1978.

Maxwell, John C. *The 21 Indispensable Qualities of a Leader.* Nashville: Thomas Nelson, Inc., 1999.

SAVING THE BEST FOR LAST

When you are putting together your essay, think about the order in which you state your points. For example, where do you want your strongest point? Should it be in your first body paragraph, your second, or your third?

The following illustration may help you decide.

THE THREE DOORS. Imagine you are in a room with three doors. Each door looks exactly the same on the outside, but each has a different number. You know that behind one of the doors is one million dollars and behind each of the other two doors is a hungry lion anxious for a snack. The problem is, you don't know which door leads to a lion and which door leads to the money.

The question is: Which door would you pick?

In classroom experimentation with this problem, 47% of students selected Door #3, well above the 27% that selected Door #1 and the 26% that selected Door #2. Clearly there is something magnetic about that third position, since random selection would tell us that the third door should be chosen only 33% of the time.

Because of the prominence of the third position, it makes sense to leave your strongest point for last when you are writing. Your reader is more likely to pay attention to the third point; your reader will also probably remember it longer than the first and second points.

Another illustration of the power of the third position comes from the business world. Sales trainers tell their students to give the customer three choices and to put the best product as the third and last choice. These trainers claim that 71% of people choose the third option.

If these illustrations don't persuade you that there is power in the third position, experiment for yourself. Do a survey of ten people, presenting them with the three-door problem. Record your results below:

THREE DOOR PROBLEM

Door #1

Door #2

Door #3

THREE-PEAT AFTER ME

DO IT NOW
Sometimes repeating the same word three times helps to attract the reader's attention. Henry James used this "three-peat" technique when he wrote, "Three things in human life are important. The first is to be kind. The second is to be kind. And the third is to be kind."

See if you can guess the repeated idea in each quote below. (Your ideas may be better than the original!)

1. Three things make you a winner in this business: _____, _____. And, of course, _____. (Harry Benson)

2. There are three things which the public will always clamor for, sooner or later: namely, _____, _____, and _____. (Thomas Hood)

3. The world rests on three things: _____, _____, and _____. (Hebrew Proverb)

4. _____, _____, and _____! The first, and last, and the middle virtue of a politician. (John Adams)

5. Dancing is just_____, _____, _____. (Martha Graham)

6. To succeed as a conjurer, three things are essential—first, _____; second, _____; and third, _____. (Robert Houdin)

7. To go to war three things must be ready: _____, _____, and once again _____. (Gian Giacomo Di Trivulzio)

DO IT NOW
Select a topic you are interested in and know something about. Write your own three-peat sentence where you emphasize a point by repeating it three times.

_____

_____

_____

_____

_____

_____

Thinking in Threes © Taylor & Francis

Permission is granted to photocopy or reproduce this page for single classroom use only.

37

SUPPORTING TOPIC SENTENCES

USE THREE TYPES OF EVIDENCE
TO SUPPORT TOPIC SENTENCES

Most people know Mahatma Gandhi as one of the great leaders in history. Here are three details you might not know about him:

1. He walked barefoot everywhere he went, so the soles of his feet were thick and hard.
2. A very religious man, he frequently fasted. As a result, he was very thin and frail.
3. He had very bad breath.

To sum up all these "facts" about Gandhi, you might say he was:

A super calloused fragile mystic plagued with halitosis.

The above joke is pure fiction, of course. In a joke you can get away with making up the facts, but in an essay you need solid evidence that will persuade your reader. As you write your essay, think like a lawyer preparing a case that will be argued before a jury. To persuade a jury that a client is not guilty, a lawyer must have specific, persuasive evidence—and plenty of it.

Three specific types of evidence will help you make your case:

1. EXAMPLES. As you write any essay, these three words should be uppermost in your mind: *Give an example!* Examples help your reader visualize what you are saying.

For example, suppose that you write, "My home town is so boring." You should follow up this general statement with an example so that your reader can see what you mean by "boring." You might write, "The streets stand empty even in the middle of the day, and young people wander the sidewalks looking for something to do."

2. FACTS (AND STATISTICS). Like examples, facts and statistics help your reader to see your point more clearly. They help persuade your reader that what you are saying is valid.

For example, suppose you tell a friend that your father was a great athlete when he was in high school. Backing up this general statement with a fact or statistic will help your friend understand what you mean by "great." You might state a fact: "My father lettered in football, basketball, and track," or, "My father was a state champion in the long jump and 100 yard dash." You could also use statistics: "My father lettered in three different sports in all four years of high school," or, "My father ran a 4:05 mile and won the state batting championship three times, with a .405 career batting average."

3. QUOTATIONS. Using quotations from experts or other knowledgeable sources can make your writing sound more authoritative. It lets your reader know that you took the time and effort to educate yourself on the topic.

Thinking in Threes © Taylor & Francis

41

Permission is granted to photocopy or reproduce this page for single classroom use only.

For example, suppose you are writing about an abstract idea like courage. You can make the subject more concrete by using an insightful quotation:

Winston Churchill said, "Courage is what it takes to stand up and speak;
courage is also what it takes to sit down and listen."

Examples, quotes, facts and statistics are not mutually exclusive. For instance, you might use a quotation as an example, or you might use a quotation with a statistic in it. The important thing is that you have specific details and evidence to back up your points.

Three specific pieces of evidence per point is a good rule of thumb. You won't always be able to manage three, but use that as your goal.

 Practice supporting a topic sentence. Select one of the topic sentences below and support it by writing a paragraph using (just this once!) *made-up* facts, quotations, and examples.

1. Bowling is a great recreational activity because it encourages physical fitness.

2. Infomercials should be banned from television because they create too much stress for viewers.

3. Less homework will make students more intelligent.

4. Ketchup is the most patriotic of all condiments.

5. *The Wizard of Oz* should be required viewing for every young person because of its lessons about the importance of teamwork.

6. The Frisbee is the best toy ever invented because of its many uses.

EXAMPLES NEED THREE QUALITIES

If you have an important point to make, don't try to be subtle or clever.
Use a pile driver. Hit the point once. Then come back and hit it again.
Then hit it a third time with a tremendous whack.

—Winston Churchill

When writing an essay, you should have plenty of examples that illustrate and support your topic sentences. However, the examples should have three important qualities:

1. **THEY SHOULD BE RELEVANT:** Because the purpose of examples is to prove your point, they should be relevant. In other words, they should relate directly to your topic sentence.

   For example, if you are arguing that television is important because it provides the public with important governmental information, don't use infomercials as an example. Infomercials have nothing to do with governmental information. Instead, you might mention the weekly city council meetings televised on a public access station.

2. **THEY SHOULD BE SPECIFIC:** Use *specific* details in your examples, such as names, dates, and places. For example, if you are writing about leadership, you might use Napoleon as an example. If you are writing about natural disasters, you might use the eruption of Mount St. Helens in 1980 as a specific example. If you are writing about good luck charms, you might mention horseshoes, rabbits' feet, and four-leaf clovers as specific examples.

3. **THEY SHOULD BE VARIED:** Try to use a *variety* of examples. For instance, if you are writing about courage, you might use a historical example *and* an example from literature or current events. You could also use an example from your personal observation or experience. A variety of examples will help keep your reader interested.

DO IT NOW Circle the examples below that are *relevant* to the topic sentence:

TOPIC SENTENCE: William Shakespeare is the most influential writer in the English language because of his amazing use of words.

1. He made up over 1,700 new words.
2. He was born in Stratford-on-Avon in 1564.
3. His words and phrases are quoted in written and spoken English more than any other single writer's.
4. No one knows exactly when and how Shakespeare died.
5. He married a woman named Anne Hathaway when he was 18.

SUPPORTING TOPIC SENTENCES

CONTINUED

DO IT NOW — One of the examples below does not support the topic sentence because it is not *specific*. Circle the sentence that is not specific.

TOPIC SENTENCE: Young people don't read newspapers because there is too much competition from television and computers.

1. Because there has been such an amazing growth in entertainment options over the past ten years, young people choose to sit in front of their computers or their televisions, rather than read newspapers.

2. Sixty-eight percent of children 8 to 18 have televisions in their rooms, and 33 percent have computers. This same group spends an average of six hours and 21 minutes a day with electronic media but just 43 minutes with print media.

3. Mary Jackson, the mother of two teenage boys and one teenage girl, commented, "My kids and all their friends never touch a newspaper. All their free time is spent watching television, listening to CDs, or playing games on their PlayStation."

DO IT NOW — Look at the two paragraph outlines below. Which outline has the most *varied* examples?

OUTLINE 1

TOPIC SENTENCE: The courage to stand up to a crowd is one trait that makes great leaders.

Example 1: Atticus, in the novel *To Kill A Mockingbird*, stands up to a lynch mob.
Example 2: Rosa Parks stood against prejudice by refusing to move to the back of the bus.
Example 3: My grandfather stood up for his friend during the civil rights movement.

OUTLINE 2

TOPIC SENTENCE: The courage to stand up to a crowd is one trait that makes great leaders.

Example 1: Ronald Reagan stood up to the Soviet Union during the Cold War.
Example 2: John F. Kennedy stood up to the Soviet Union during the Cuban Missile Crisis.
Example 3: George Washington stood up against England during the American Revolution.

THREE THINGS
TO INCLUDE IN A QUOTATION

If you use quotations to support your topic sentences, be sure to integrate them smoothly into your paper. Don't make the mistake of padding your paper with too many quotes or simply tacking them into your paper without any explanation.

Integrate quotations into your paper by including these three things:

1. **A TRANSITION.** A transitional word or phrase, such as "for example," "according to," or "as stated by" lets the reader know that a quote is coming.

2. **A LEAD-IN.** A lead-in identifies the speaker and his or her title or qualifications. It tells the reader something about the credibility of your source. (If the source is not a person, the lead-in should give the name of the group or organization responsible.)

3. **A PARENTHETICAL REFERENCE.** A parenthetical reference tells the reader, in parentheses, the author's name and the page number where you found the quotation. A Works Cited section at the end of your paper will give the rest of the information—for example, the name of the book, the publisher, the date of publication, etc.

Below is an example of a quotation that has all three of the elements above. It is taken from an essay that argues the importance of improving vocabulary.

For example, Larry Krieger, author of *Mastering the Verbal SAT* says, "The textbooks, primary sources, and novels you read in school are replete with SAT words." (Krieger 44).

The quotation uses a transition: *for example*. It has a lead-in identifying the speaker: *Larry Krieger, author of Mastering the Verbal SAT*. (The fact that Larry Krieger is the author of a book on the verbal SAT lets the reader know that he qualifies as an authority on the topic.) It includes a parenthetical reference telling the source of the quote: (Krieger 44).

Sometimes you may want to quote someone but not use *all* of their words. To leave out a part of the quote, use an *ellipsis* instead of the words you are leaving out. To make an ellipsis, type three periods (. . .).

QUOTE WITH AN ELLIPSIS

According to Mark Fenton, editor of the Boston-based *Walking Magazine*, the benefits of walking are immense: "We see again and again that regular exercise gives an improved sense of self-worth and an improved sense of purpose . . . It's also clear that regular activity may reduce the likelihood of clinical depression" (Walking as a Way of Life).

To add material to a quote to clarify its meaning, put brackets ([ ]) around any words that you add.

QUOTE WITH BRACKETS

U.S. Congresswoman Susan A. Davis praises Tony, saying, "[He] is living proof that if you work hard you can achieve almost anything" (Davis).

MORE ABOUT QUOTATIONS

When using quotations, writers should understand the difference between a direct quote and an indirect quote, and the difference between a long quote and a short quote.

DIRECT QUOTES AND INDIRECT QUOTES. A direct quote uses someone's *exact* words, with quotation marks. An indirect quote tells what someone said, but *without* using the exact words. No quotation marks are used with an indirect quote.

Here are examples of direct and indirect quotes. Notice that both examples identify the original source of the quotation. (More detailed information would be in the "Works Cited" section at the end of the paper.)

DIRECT QUOTE

For example, according to Anjetta McQueen, an education writer, "About 36 percent of high school graduates do not go straight to college, even though a college graduate's earning power over a lifetime is nearly twice that of a high school graduate" (McQueen C4).

INDIRECT QUOTE

For example, according to Anjetta McQueen, an education writer, although the economic benefits of college seem obvious, about one third of graduates of high school do not enroll in college (McQueen C4).

SHORT QUOTES AND LONG QUOTES:

A short quote is four lines or fewer in length. It is punctuated with quotation marks. A long quote is five lines or more in length. It uses indentation instead of quotation marks to indicate that it is a quote.

Here is an example of a long quote:

The poet Donald Hall argues that reading aloud and recitation are vital components for building fluent readers:

> If when we read silently we do not hear a text, we slide past words passively, without making decisions, without knowing or caring…We might as well be watching haircuts or "Conan the Barbarian." In the old Out-Loud Culture, print was always potential speech; even silent readers, too shy to read aloud, inwardly heard the sound of words. Their culture identified print and voice. Everyone's ability to read was enhanced by recitation. Then we read aggressively; then we demanded sense (Hall 12).

PRACTICE WITH QUOTATIONS

DO IT NOW

Read the paragraph below and do the following:
1. Label each direct quote as "DQ" and each indirect quote as "IQ."
2. Label each short quote "SQ" and each long quote "LQ."
3. Underline the lead-ins before each quote.

The ability to focus is one of the most important traits of successful individuals. One example of an individual who obtained success through focus is professional baseball player Tony Gwynn. To become a professional baseball player, an athlete needs a number of skills, but not every skill can be a player's strength. Tony Gwynn devoted himself to his strength: the art of hitting. He read and re-read Ted William's book *The Science of Hitting*. He viewed countless hours of videotape at home and on the road, studying his swing to make it as perfect as possible. He constantly talked about hitting with his teammates and anyone else who had expertise. Even when he wasn't playing baseball, he would do some kind of activity, such as playing Ping-Pong, that would improve his hand-eye coordination. Tony's focus earned him eight batting titles and a tremendous lifetime batting average of .339 (Maxwell 56). Mike Lopresti, sportswriter for *USA Today,* says that the most amazing statistic that shows Gwynn's amazing hitting is the fact that he struck out twice in a single game only 32 times in his 20-year professional baseball career (Lopresti 12). U.S. Congresswoman Susan A. Davis praises Tony saying, "[He] is living proof that if you work hard you can achieve almost anything" (Davis 53). Good concentration, however, is not a skill just for professional athletes. Leadership expert and author John C. Maxwell tells the following anecdote to illustrate the importance of focus for everyone:

> Experienced animal trainers take a stool with them when they step into a cage with a lion. Why a stool? It tames a lion better than anything—except maybe a tranquilizer gun. When the trainer holds the stool with the legs extended toward the lion's face, the animal tries to focus on all four legs at once. And that paralyzes him. Divided focus always works against you (Maxwell 57).

Successful individuals in many walks of life or professions are those who are able to identify strengths and to focus on improving them.

WORKS CITED

Davis, Susan A. "Say it isn't so, Tony." 3 Oct. 2001. U.S. House of Representatives. 3 May 2005 http://www.house.gov/susandavis/editorials/ed100301tonygwynn.html.

Lopresti, Mike. "Gwynn: Subtle Skills, Hall of Fame Numbers." *USA Today*. 28 June 2001.

Maxwell, John C. *The 21 Indispensable Qualities of a Leader*. Nashville: Thomas Nelson, Inc. 1999.

Thinking in Threes © Taylor & Francis

Permission is granted to photocopy or reproduce this page for single classroom use only.

47

HALL OF FAME

To support your topic sentences, use three types of evidence:
examples, facts, and quotations.

DO IT NOW Complete the items below:

1. Select a famous person you would put in your personal hall of fame. It should be a person whose life and achievements have inspired or influenced you in some way.

    Example: *Thomas Alva Edison*

    YOUR SELECTION:

    _____

2. What are three qualities of the person that make him/her inspirational or influential? Use adjectives to describe these qualities.

    Example: *creative, hardworking, positive*

    ADJECTIVES FOR YOUR PERSON:

    _____

3. For each quality, give examples of how the person demonstrated the quality through his/her life and achievements. As you select examples, make sure they are relevant to qualification for your hall of fame. Also make sure they are as specific as possible. Finally, try for a variety of examples.

    Examples of how Edison was creative:
    *   *He created more than one thousand inventions.*
    *   *He invented the idea of the large research laboratory.*

    EXAMPLES OF YOUR PERSON'S FIRST QUALITY:

    _____

    _____

    _____

    Examples of how Edison was hardworking:
    *   *He worked continually until his death at age 84.*
    *   *Even though it took over ten thousand tries to find the correct materials for the incandescent light bulb, he did not give up until he found the answer.*

CONTINUED

EXAMPLES OF YOUR PERSON'S SECOND QUALITY:

_____

_____

_____

Examples of how Edison was positive:
- *After his laboratory burned down in 1914, he rebuilt it and continued to work for another seventeen years.*
- *Even though he had little education and suffered from deafness, he continued to achieve his goals.*

EXAMPLES OF YOUR PERSON'S THIRD QUALITY:

_____

_____

_____

4. Research some facts and statistics about your selection. Try to select facts and statistics that will help you show how your person was inspirational and influential.

Example:
- *Edison patented the phonograph in 1877.*
- *He patented the incandescent light bulb in 1879.*
- *He held a total of 1,093 patents.*
- *His formal schooling was limited to three months.*
- *He established the first permanent central electric-light power plant in the world.*
- *The research laboratory he established and organized eventually became the General Electric Company.*
- *He died at age 84 in 1931.*

FACTS AND STATISTICS ABOUT YOUR PERSON:

_____

_____

_____

5. Research some quotations that you might use to persuade your audience that the person is inspiring or influential. Make sure to document the source of each quotation.

Examples:
- According to historian Michael Hart, "For most of his life, Edison suffered from seriously impaired hearing. However, he more than compensated for that handicap by his astonishing capacity for hard work" (Hart 56).
- Thomas Edison: "Genius is ninety-nine percent perspiration and one percent inspiration."

- Thomas Edison: "Many of life's failures are people who did not realize how close they were to success when they gave up."

According to leadership expert John C. Maxwell:

> The lab [Edison] built in West Orange, New Jersey, was world famous. He called the fourteen-building complex his invention factory. Its main building was massive—greater than three football fields in size. From that base of operations, he and his staff conceived of inventions, developed prototypes, manufactured products and shipped them to customers. It became a model for modern research and manufacturing (Maxwell 90).

QUOTATIONS BY OR ABOUT YOUR PERSON:

_____

_____

_____

_____

_____

_____

_____

_____

_____

_____

_____

_____

_____

_____

_____

_____

_____

_____

_____

_____

CALLING THE GAME

> *A sad woman walked along a deserted beach. As she walked, she kicked at the sand, lost in melancholy thought. Suddenly she saw a flash of silver in the sand and pulled up a genie's silver lamp. As she brushed off the sand, a large plume of smoke rose from the lamp, and a genie appeared.*
>
> *"You have released me from prison," said the genie. "To reward you, I will grant you three wishes, but you must also realize that your mate will receive double what you request."*
>
> *The woman protested, "But my husband is a jerk! He just left me for another woman!"*
>
> *"I am sorry," answered the genie. "Those are the ground rules."*
>
> *"Okay, for my first wish I would like a million dollars, and for my second wish I would like a 30-room mansion on this beachfront property," said the woman.*
>
> *Immediately, a pile of money appeared at the woman's feet and a beautiful 30-room mansion appeared on the vacant lot along the beach. "So, you are telling me," said the woman, "that my husband has a pile of money twice as large as mine and a 60-room mansion?"*
>
> *"Yes, that is correct," said the genie, "What is your third wish?"*
>
> *The woman thought carefully. Her frustrated expression suddenly transformed into a huge grin as she came up with a fiendishly clever idea.*
>
> *"For my third wish," the woman said gleefully, "I want you to scare me half to death!"*

The punch line of the above story—"Scare me half to death"—does not work unless the writer has set everything else in place. The characters, the setting, the facts, and the explanations must all be clear.

An essay is no different. The writer must set everything in place in order to persuade the reader.

One way to make everything clear for the reader is to write as though you are a combination of a play-by-play commentator and a color commentator for a televised sporting event. The play-by-play commentator's job is to relay the facts and statistics—what exactly is happening on the field throughout the game. For example, a football play-by-play commentator will tell you where exactly the ball is on the field and how far the offense has to go to get a first down. He might also tell you how many first downs the two teams have had in the game so far.

The color commentator's job is to interpret and explain the facts and statistics. He tries to give the meaning behind the facts and figures. For example, if it's the fourth quarter and the home team has had only one first down, the color commentator will probably explain that the failure to get first downs has contributed to the home team's low score.

As a writer explaining and proving a thesis, you must do the job of both the play-by-play commentator and the color commentator. Your first job is to clearly state the point. Your second job is to provide the evidence that proves your point, giving specific examples, facts, and details.

You must also do a *third* job: provide the color commentary that interprets and explains the evidence and relates it back to your thesis. In practical terms, that means that each piece of evidence should be followed by at least one or two sentences of explanation. You must explain *how* the evidence helps prove your point.

CONTINUED

Read the paragraph below to see if the writer has done all three of his or her jobs: making a point, providing the evidence to prove that point (the play-by-play), and interpreting and explaining the evidence (the color commentary).

1. Circle the main point of the paragraph: the topic sentence.
2. Put brackets [ ] around the evidence: the play-by-play.
3. Underline the explanation: the color commentary.

When it comes to efficiency of communication, e-mail has several advantages over the telephone. Surveys by market researcher Meta Group found that 82.8% of people cited the ability to communicate with multiple parties via e-mail to be its most important advantage (Flash C5). Not only can business people communicate with many people at the same time, they can also communicate more rapidly. There are no busy signals with e-mail and you don't have to worry about interrupting someone's dinner or their sleep. Another factor that makes e-mail efficient is the fact that it creates a paper trail. Lorelle Smith, a web site designer, explained why getting things in writing is so important: "About a year ago I decided I wanted to encourage people to use e-mail because I wanted that written record of what they want so I have that legally. And I want them to write out their question instead of wasting my time." Because e-mail records the times and dates of communication and the exact words that were exchanged, it is an easy and efficient way to create a communication archive. Alyssa Agee, a document manager at a technology-consulting company says that she feels more articulate when she writes. Also, she likes the money she saves by not having to pay long distance charges (Flash C5). In allowing communication that is more flexible, more rapid, clearer, and cheaper, e-mail is clearly superior to the telephone.

WORK CITED

Flash, Cynthia. "Phone vs. E-mail: Communicating a Preference." *The Seattle Times*. 23 June 2003: C5.

WORN OUT WORDS

Clichés are trite, overused expressions like "hungry as a bear" or "quiet as a mouse." Because your reader has seen and heard them so many times, they don't carry much punch. If you find yourself using a cliché, just try putting the idea into your own words rather than using a prefabricated phrase that you've heard 100 times.

    Clichés often, though not always, happen to be three-word phrases. Below are a number of examples of three-word clichés.

all washed up	hope against hope	off his rocker
at death's door	in seventh heaven	over the hill
behind the times	jump the gun	pave the way
bury the hatchet	jump for joy	play second fiddle
chew the fat	kick the bucket	reinvent the wheel
fair weather fan	larger than life	run the gauntlet
feast or famine	make ends meet	save the day
first things first	mind over matter	scared to death
go to town	on cloud nine	take a hike
good as gold	on a roll	thanks a million
hit rock bottom	on thin ice	under the gun
hit the hay	out to lunch	

DO IT NOW   Use the clues below to complete the following three-word clichés:

1. trying to meet a deadline: *under* _____ _____.
2. be very happy: *jump* _____ _____.
3. go to sleep: *hit* _____ _____.
4. old: *over* _____ _____.
5. using your brain power to overcome an obstacle: *mind* _____ _____.
6. starting too soon: *jump* _____ _____.
7. things are either going very well or very bad: *feast* _____ _____.
8. not paying attention: *out* _____ _____.
9. to survive with the necessary resources: *make* _____ _____.
10. forget past grievances: *bury* _____ _____.

DO IT NOW   Write a sentence using each of the three-word clichés, above. Then rewrite the sentence completely, getting rid of the three-word cliché and trying to express the same meaning in a more original way.

Example:
1. Bob was tense because he was *under the gun* to get his research paper finished by Friday. Bob felt as though he were nearing the edge of a cliff and about to plummet into a canyon—all because of the pressure to get his research paper finished by Friday.

WRITING INTRODUCTIONS

THREE WAYS TO "HOOK"
THE READER

> *In an ancient story, the city of Thebes was tormented by a monster with the body of a lion and the upper torso of a woman. The monster, known as the Sphinx, lay on the top of a rock along the roadside and challenged travelers with a riddle. Those who solved the riddle were allowed to pass, but those who failed were killed.*
>
> *Undaunted by the failure of every one of his predecessors, the hero Oedipus stepped forward bravely to take the challenge. The Sphinx asked, "What animal goes on four feet in the morning, on two at noon, and on three in the evening?"*
>
> *Undaunted, Oedipus replied, "Man. In childhood, he creeps on hands and knees. In manhood, he walks erect. In old age, he walks with the aid of a staff."*
>
> *Mortified by Oedipus' correct answer, the Sphinx cast herself down from the rock and perished.*

When presented with a riddle like the one in the anecdote above, it is human nature to want to know the answer. As a writer, you too can capitalize on human curiosity to compel your reader to read on. There are many techniques that will get your essay off to a great start for both you and your reader.

Imagine that a student is given this writing assignment: *If you had to eat one food every day, what would it be?* She thinks for a moment and writes, *I would like to eat hamburgers every day because they are good.*

This beginning does not exactly inspire the reader to read on. Worse, it provides little for the writer herself to get excited about. It does answer the question, and it does provide a focus for a possible composition, but the weak opening provides little promise for much else.

Here are three tips the writer could have used to write a more interesting introduction:

1. Begin with *conflict.*
2. Begin with *mystery.*
3. Begin with *metaphor.*

First impressions are important. A good "hook" in the introduction will grab your reader's interest. It will also help you, the writer, think creatively and produce more than just a dull, ordinary essay.

 **DO IT NOW** For each essay question listed below, two introductory sentences are provided. Circle the letter (A or B) that you think makes the most interesting hook.

1. QUESTION: What section of the newspaper do you think is the most important to read?

A. My brother and I always fight over the sports section. While reading the paper I always sit with my back to a wall to avoid an unexpected attack.

B. The section of the newspaper I like to read is the sports section.

2. QUESTION: What are things a person should not do during a speech?

   A. *When giving a speech, you should never have gum in your mouth.*

   B. *In surveys taken about people's biggest fears, fear of giving a speech often rates above fear of death.*

3. QUESTION: What is your favorite book? What are the reasons everyone should read it?

   A. *Groucho Marx once said, "Outside of a dog, a book is man's best friend; inside of a dog it's too dark to read anyway."*

   B. *Books are a very important part of many people's lives.*

4. QUESTION: If you had to eat one food every day, what would it be?

   A. *I really like pizza.*

   B. *Pizza is a lifesaver in an ocean of bland food choices; it buoys me up in a sea of crummy cuisine.*

BEGINNING WITH CONFLICT

*Three ways to hook your reader: with conflict,
with mystery, or with metaphor.*

Human beings love conflict. If you have ever seen the way heads turn in a public place when two or more people raise their voices in anger at each other, you've witnessed firsthand how conflict attracts attention. At the root of every story, whether fiction or nonfiction, is some kind of conflict. It may be an *internal conflict*, as when a character is struggling about whether or not to tell someone the truth. It may also be an *external conflict*, as when two neighbors are battling about a fence, or a hiker is battling an unexpected snowstorm.

Opening your essay with a conflict taps into your readers' innate curiosity. It also forces you to write about specific and concrete people, places, and things.

Examples:

QUESTION: *If you had to eat one food every day, what would it be?*

CONFLICT HOOK: *My family always gets into an argument when we try to decide what kind of pizza to order.*

QUESTION: *What one section of the newspaper do you think is the most important to read?*

CONFLICT HOOK: *My brother and I always fight over the sports section of the newspaper. While reading the paper, I always sit with my back to a wall to avoid an unexpected attack.*

DO IT NOW Select three of the questions below, and write a conflict hook of at least one complete sentence for each.

1. What are some things about your hometown that you might mention to promote tourism?

2. What are some things that you like about your favorite movie or television program?

3. Who do you think is the most influential person in history? What are the reasons he/she is influential?

4. What are the qualities that make an effective leader?

5. What is your favorite book? What are the reasons everyone should read it?

BEGINNING WITH MYSTERY

*Three ways to hook your reader: with conflict,
with mystery, or with metaphor.*

Like a good game of poker, the key to using a "mystery" hook is not to show your hand too soon. In other words, you delay telling the reader what your topic is. You want your reader to *want* to read on, to *need* to read on.

The simple technique for writing this kind of introduction is to use pronouns instead of the name of your topic, until the end of the introduction. Here are two examples:

It's the kind of food you could eat every day of the year and twice on Monday. It's the kind of food that is impossible to cook badly. It's the kind of food that even fussy children never complain about. If you haven't guessed by now, this essential food is pizza.

Without this section of the newspaper, I could not start my morning. I would be without conversation topics for the day. I would have nothing funny to tape in my notebook or inside my locker. I would not be able to start my day with a smile. What is this vital section of the newspaper? It's the comics, of course.

DO IT NOW Select one of the questions below and write an introduction with a mystery hook.

1. What are some things about your hometown that you might mention to promote tourism?

2. What are some things that you like about your favorite movie or television program?

3. Who do you think is the most influential person in history? What are the reasons he/she is influential?

4. What are the qualities that make an effective leader?

5. What is your favorite book? What are the reasons everyone should read it?

BEGINNING WITH METAPHOR

*Three ways to hook your reader: with conflict,
with mystery, or with metaphor.*

A *metaphor* is a comparison of two unlike things. For example, here is a metaphor that compares *success* to a *fish*:

Success is a fish that is elusive and difficult to catch, swimming in the murky depths of the future.

Metaphors can help both you and your readers to see things in a new way. When you use a metaphor in your introduction, readers quickly see that you are not using a boring approach to your topic. Even if they don't necessarily agree with your comparison, they will be interested enough to keep reading.

Here are three examples of metaphors about the topic of "words":

Words are legs.
Words are corn.
Words are circus animals.

The three metaphors above are not quite complete and don't really make much sense. It is the writer's responsibility to make the connection between the two unlike nouns. In other words, the writer must *make* the strange comparison make sense.

Below, the three metaphors have been completed. The writers have taken two things that seem to have no relationship whatsoever and made a connection that helps readers to see "words" in a new way.

Words are the legs of the mind; they bear it about, carry it from point to point, bed it down at night, and keep it off the ground and out of the marsh and mists. (Richard Eder)

Language is a growing thing that, like a corn crop, has many uses. As a staple, corn feeds people, horses, and hogs; language also serves utilitarian ends. As a colorless liquid, corn intoxicates. So does language, fermented in a sermon, distilled in a song or a story. Corn was made for people, not the other way around. So too with language. (Jim Wayne Miller)

Words are as recalcitrant as circus animals, and the unskilled trainer can crack his whip at them in vain. (Gerald Brenan)

To create metaphors, practice the three-step process that follows. If you keep at it, you'll discover that the human mind has an amazing ability to hold onto two contradictory ideas at the same time and manipulate the two ideas so that they become remarkably similar.

HOW TO CREATE A METAPHOR IN THREE EASY STEPS:

STEP 1. Begin with your topic.

Example: *Monday*

STEP 2: Compare your topic to another unrelated noun.

Example: *Monday is a soup.*

STEP 3: Connect the two topics. Elaborate by answering *Who? What? When? Where? Why?* or *How?*

Example: *Monday is a thick, spicy soup that's hard to swallow, but its nourishing stock fortifies us for the week.*

MORE ON FIGURATIVE LANGUAGE

In addition to metaphor, there are two other types of figurative language that you might use to introduce your essay: *simile* and *personification*.

SIMILE. A simile is like a metaphor except that it uses the words *like* or *as* to compare two unlike things.

Example: *Pizza is like a sunny summer afternoon at the lake; it's never an unpleasant experience.*

PERSONIFICATION. Personification refers to describing an animal, object, or idea as if it were a person. To create personification, you must first select words that are normally used to describe a person or a person's actions. Then use these words to describe the animal, object, or idea.

Examples:
- *Procrastination always causes problems that jump out of the bushes to scare you when you least expect it.*
- *Monday morning always arrives at your door too early and raps loudly until you are forced to get up and acknowledge its existence.*

Like metaphors, similes and personification are effective as tools to introduce your topic because they force you and your reader to look at the topic in a new and different way. (You can also use figurative language anywhere else in your writing; it's not just for introductions.)

DO IT NOW Select one of the questions below and write an introduction with a hook that contains a metaphor, a simile, or personification.

1. What are the things about you that make you unique?

2. What are some things about your hometown that you might mention to promote tourism?

3. What are some things that you like about your favorite movie or television program?

4. Who do you think is the most influential person in history? What are the reasons he/she is influential?

5. What are things a person should not do during a speech?

THREE MORE WAYS
TO "HOOK" THE READER

Using conflict, mystery, and metaphor are not the only ways to begin a composition. Here are three other possible alternatives:

ANECDOTE HOOK. The anecdote hook relies on a story to hook the reader. Because people like stories, using a specific, short anecdote is a great way to capture your reader's interest.

For example, if you are writing about public speaking or Thanksgiving, you might relate an anecdote about former Secretary of State William M. Evarts. He began a Thanksgiving dinner speech by saying, "You have been giving your attention to a turkey stuffed with sage; you are now about to consider a sage stuffed with turkey."

STARTLING FACT OR STATISTIC. Another good hook is a startling fact or statistic that captures the curiosity of your reader.

Example:
Each year, major league baseball uses the skins of 45,000 cows to create its baseballs. Can that many cows be wrong? No way!

QUOTATION HOOK. An interesting or humorous quotation that relates to your topic is a good way to hook your reader. For example, if you were writing about one of your favorite books, you might use this quote by Groucho Marx: "Outside of a dog, a book is man's best friend; inside of a dog it's too dark to read anyway."

 **DO IT NOW** — Select one or more of the questions below. Then write three different introductory "hooks": one with an anecdote, one with a startling fact or statistic, and one with a quotation.

1. Why should children have pets?

2. What are some alternative uses for a newspaper, besides reading it?

3. What are ways to be kind on a daily basis?

4. What are the qualities that make an effective leader?

5. What is your favorite book? What are the reasons everyone should read it?

YET THREE MORE WAYS
TO "HOOK" THE READER

Conflict, mystery, and metaphor can be used in an introduction to "hook" the reader. So can anecdotes, startling facts or statistics, and quotations. Here are three *more* ways to hook your reader's interest:

HYPERBOLE HOOK: Hyperbole is the use of exaggeration for effect. To create this kind of hook, just think of an unusual or exaggerated claim that you can make about your topic. (Of course, after you make your claim, you will have to go on and explain it or defend it!)

Examples:

- *Pizza is and always has been the secret to high intelligence.*

- *I would prefer eating a pound of lard to getting up early on a Monday morning.*

BIZARRE IMAGE HOOK: Use descriptive language and imagery to paint a picture that is strange enough to capture your reader's attention:

Examples:

- *If I had my wish, I would be buried in a giant vat of pizza sauce.*

- *Visiting the Tupperware Museum Gallery of Historical Food Containers is not exactly my idea of an exciting vacation.*

COUNTERING CONVENTIONAL WISDOM HOOK. To use this hook, simply think about what your audience is expecting to hear about your topic; then, say something else. By going against what people normally say, you are bound to say something new and interesting. For example, if you are writing about the reasons you like pizza, your audience expects you to talk about the pizza itself: the crust and the toppings. But to counter conventional wisdom, you must think differently. For example, you might say, "The most important ingredient in a good pizza is on-time delivery." Of course, you still must write a thesis that goes along with your hook. If you don't really think that on-time delivery is the most important part of a pizza, you should try another type of hook.

DO IT NOW Using one or more of the questions below, write an introductory hook based on hyperbole, an introductory hook based on a bizarre image, and an introductory hook that counters conventional wisdom.

1. Should children have pets?

2. What are some alternative uses for a newspaper, besides reading it?

3. What are ways to be kind on a daily basis?

4. What are the qualities that make an effective leader?

5. What is your favorite book? What are the reasons everyone should read it?

QUOTES WITH THREE

Great writers know the power of three. Each of the quotes below talks about three ideas. One of the ideas, however, is missing. How would *you* complete each of these quotations? (Even if you know the original, see if you can complete it in a different way.)

1. There are three classes of people: lovers of wisdom, lovers of humor, and lovers of
   _____. (Plato)

2. My father gave me three hints in public speaking: be sincere, be brief, and be
   _____.(James Roosevelt)

3. The three basic definitions of science:
   If it's green or wiggles, it's biology.
   If it stinks, it's chemistry.
   If it doesn't work, it's _____. (Timothy J. Rolfe)

4. In every negotiation, three crucial elements are always present—information, time, and
   _____. (Herb Cohen)

5. There are three periods in life: youth, middle age, and "how well you _____."
   (Nelson Rockefeller)

6. There exist only three beings worthy of respect: the priest, the soldier, the poet. To know,
   to kill, to _____. (Charles Baudelaire)

7. Folks are serious about three things—their religion, their family, and, most of all, their
   _____. (Bert Lance)

8. There are three parts in truth: first, the inquiry, which is the wooing of it; secondly, the
   knowledge of it, which is the presence of it; and thirdly, the _____,
   which is the enjoyment of it. (Francis Bacon)

WRITING FLUENT SENTENCES

THREE WAYS TO WRITE FLUENT SENTENCES

It's impossible to write an effective essay or even a good paragraph without writing fluent sentences. Fluent sentences are sentences that are clear, concise, and correct. They fit together well and flow easily. Here are three ways to write smooth sentences:

USE A VARIETY OF SENTENCE OPENINGS. Not every sentence should begin with a subject. Starting sentences in different ways will help your writing flow smoothly. When every sentence begins the same way, a writer's work can sound lifeless, immature, and boring.

USE A VARIETY OF SENTENCE LENGTHS. Write some short sentences. Write some long sentences. Don't make them all the same. This is not interesting. This is monotonous. This is boring. Do you get the idea?

There is nothing wrong with a few short sentences, but it is important to combine some of your ideas, making sentences that have a variety of lengths. This will make your writing sound more natural, more varied, and more interesting.

USE PARALLELISM. Which is better?

I came. Then I saw. Then I conquered.

or

I came, I saw, I conquered.

The second example, the words supposedly spoken by Julius Caesar after a victory, is stronger because of the *parallelism*. Each set of three sentences has the exact same structure, creating a smooth, balanced, and rhythmic sound.

You don't want to make every sentence parallel—that would be overdoing it. Instead, use parallelism occasionally to add style and punch to your writing.

 **DO IT NOW** Rewrite the paragraph below, using a variety of sentences and a variety of sentence openings. You may combine sentences and eliminate words, but don't eliminate key ideas. Try to use parallelism at least once.

Paper clips are the most amazing office product ever invented. Paper clips are useful. Paper clips are easy to use. Paper clips are fun. Paper clips are not like staples. You don't need a special device to attach them. You don't need to struggle to remove them. Paper clips can easily slip over a bundle of papers. Paper clips keep the papers bound together firmly and neatly. Paper clips can be removed with one easy motion. Paper clips can also be used for cheap entertainment. You can bend them into animal shapes. You can string them together into long chains. You can hold competitions. At the competition you can give each contestant five paper clips. The winner of the competition is the one who makes the most impressive sculpture. Paper clips are simple, malleable pieces of metal. But paper clips are really much more.

Thinking in Threes © Taylor & Francis

Permission is granted to photocopy or reproduce this page for single classroom use only.

69

SENTENCE VARIETY

Three ways to write fluent sentences: Use variety in sentence openings, variety in sentence lengths, and parallelism.

To avoid monotony in your writing, vary the openings of your sentences. Many writers naturally begin sentences with the subject, at least in their first draft. Starting with the subject is a natural feature of English sentences, and there is nothing wrong with it. However, if every one of your sentences begins with the subject, your writing will sound monotonous and lifeless.

Here are a number of options for starting a sentence with something besides the subject:

OPEN WITH ADVERBS

Original sentence, opening with the subject: *The angry shopper steered his shopping cart swiftly and forcefully through the cold cereal aisle.*

Revised sentence, opening with adverbs: *Swiftly and forcefully, the angry shopper steered his shopping cart through the cold cereal aisle.*

OPEN WITH ADJECTIVES

Original sentence, opening with the subject: *The janitor, bossy and loud, ordered the students to stop eating in the hall.*

Revised sentence, opening with adjectives: *Bossy and loud, the janitor ordered the students to stop eating in the hall.*

OPEN WITH A PREPOSITIONAL PHRASE

Original sentence, opening with the subject: *The students gathered in the cafeteria to watch the multimedia presentation on dental hygiene.*

Revised sentence, opening with a prepositional phrase: *In the cafeteria, the students gathered to watch the multimedia presentation on dental hygiene.*

OPEN WITH A PARTICIPIAL PHRASE

Original sentence, opening with the subject: *Bill killed time waiting for his dentist appointment by reading a magazine article on effective flossing techniques.*

Revised sentence, opening with a participial phrase: *Reading a magazine article on effective flossing techniques, Bill killed time waiting for his dentist appointment.*

OPEN WITH AN INFINITIVE

Original sentence, opening with the subject: *Sheila wanted to improve her bowling, so she bought a pair of expensive bowling shoes.*

Revised sentence, opening with an infinitive: *To improve her bowling, Sheila bought an expensive pair of bowling shoes.*

CONTINUED

OPEN WITH A DEPENDENT CLAUSE

Original sentence, opening with the subject: *Max likes to play Ping-Pong, so he never leaves home without his paddle.*

Original sentence, opening with a dependent clause: *Because Max likes to play Ping-Pong, he never leaves home without his paddle.*

DO IT NOW Directions: Revise the sentences below so that they begin with the designated opening.

1. The students were eager and restless as they listened by the radio to find out whether or not school had been cancelled because of the snowstorm. (Open with an adjective.)

_____

_____

2. Paul's mother told him loudly and clearly to keep the toilet seat down. (Open with an adverb.)

_____

_____

3. Mary thought about how to finish her project. She sat in the living room. (Open with a participial phrase.)

_____

_____

4. Josh ran a record mile in his sweaty bowling shoes. (Open with a prepositional phrase.)

_____

_____

5. Bill read an extra hour each night in order to improve his grades. (Open with an infinitive phrase.)

_____

_____

6. The teacher announced that the test was cancelled. The class cheered. (Open with a dependent clause.)

_____

_____

Thinking in Threes © Taylor & Francis

Permission is granted to photocopy or reproduce this page for single classroom use only.

71

VARIETY IN SENTENCE LENGTHS

Three ways to write fluent sentences: Use variety in sentence openings, variety in sentence lengths, and parallelism.

the lengths of your sentences. Sentences in English can be strung together and rearranged in a seemingly endless variety of ways. The key is to find a clear, concise, and correct combination.

There is nothing wrong with a short sentence, but too many short sentences strung together will make your writing monotonous and choppy. Likewise, too many long sentences strung together can be confusing. The idea is to strike a balance.

The three categories of connecting words, below, can help you connect sentences to add variety in length. Don't be intimidated by the technical sounding names of these connecting words; instead, just pay attention to *how* the words are used to connect sentences.

CONNECTING WORDS

- Subordinating conjunctions: *after, although, as, because, before, even though, if, since, unless, until, when, while*
- Coordinating conjunctions: *for, and, nor, but, or, yet, so*
- Conjunctive adverbs: *also, as a result, consequently, for example, furthermore, however, still, then, therefore, thus*

Below are some examples of how connecting words can be used to combine sentences. The connecting words are underlined.

EXAMPLE 1:

Sentence 1:   *The jury didn't believe the woman.*

Sentence 2:   *The woman said that she killed her husband to prevent aliens from torturing him.*

Combined
  sentence: *<u>When</u> the women said that she killed her husband to prevent aliens from torturing him, the jury didn't believe her.*

EXAMPLE 2:

Sentence 1:   *Bill is taking October 4th off from work.*

Sentence 2:   *October 4th is the anniversary of the television premier of "Leave It To Beaver."*

Combined
  sentence: *Bill is taking October 4th off from work, <u>for</u> it's the anniversary of the television premiere of "Leave It To Beaver."*

EXAMPLE 3:

Sentence 1:   *The United States leads the world in hot dog sales.*

Sentence 2:   *The United States is not even in the top 10 in mustard sales.*

Combined
  sentence: *The United States leads the world in hot dog sales; <u>however</u>, it is not even in the top 10 in mustard sales.*

CONTINUED

DO IT NOW | Follow the directions below to transform the simple sentences into a single sentence using the category of connecting words suggested.

1. Use a subordinating conjunction to combine the two sentences into a single sentence: *Pedro spent all night on it. He was unable to finish the project.*

    _____

    _____

2. Use a coordinating conjunction to combine the two sentences into a single sentence: *Sheila spent three hours writing her essay. She didn't spend any time proofreading her essay.*

    _____

    _____

    _____

3. Use a conjunctive adverb to combine the two sentences into a single sentence: *Our neighborhood ice-cream man is a big Elvis fan. His ice-cream truck plays a medley of Elvis tunes.*

    _____

    _____

    _____

Thinking in Threes © Taylor & Francis

Permission is granted to photocopy or reproduce this page for single classroom use only.

73

PARALLELISM

*Three ways to write fluent sentences: Use variety in sentence
openings, variety in sentence lengths, and parallelism.*

When Abraham Lincoln wanted to conclude his Gettysburg Address with a memorable punch, he turned to parallelism, saying:

"...this government of the people, by the people, for the people, shall not perish from this Earth."

Parallelism is more than simply the repetition of words; it's the repetition of word patterns. In Lincoln's conclusion you hear the repetition of the word *people*, but you should also hear the repetition of the prepositional phrases beginning with *of, by,* and *for.*

Parallelism is a big word for a simple concept. Our brains naturally work to recognize patterns and our ears appreciate rhythm. Using parallelism in every sentence you write would be overdoing it, but if you use parallel structure in some of your sentences, you will add a stylistic flair that will make your writing more interesting.

Notice how the following sentences employ parallelism in a variety of ways:

Early to bed, and early to rise, makes a man healthy, wealthy, and wise. (Ben Franklin)

Work saves us from three great evils: boredom, vice, and need. (Voltaire)

Tell me and I'll forget; show me and I may remember; involve me and I'll understand. (Chinese proverb)

DO IT NOW Combine each of the following groups into a single sentence, using parallel structures.

1. I am the kind of person who loves to listen to music. I also love to shop for music and to play music.

   _____

   _____

   _____

2. Joe enjoys flossing before breakfast and after dinner. He also enjoys flossing during lunch.

   _____

   _____

   _____

3. Before I slipped in the shower and broke my leg, I climbed Mount Everest. I also ran a marathon and built a log home.

_____

_____

_____

4. I studied my notes. I read my textbook. I wrote multiple drafts of my essays. I was determined to improve my grades.

_____

_____

_____

5. A good paper carrier needs to have three things. He needs a strong back. He needs an accurate aim. And he needs a strong arm.

_____

_____

_____

PARALLELISM IN ACTION

DO IT NOW The incomplete quotations below are examples of how great writers have used parallelism in their sentences. Complete each quotation in a way that retains its parallelism and makes sense. Then compare your quotations with the originals.

1. Travel is fatal to _____, bigotry, and narrow-mindedness. (Mark Twain)

2. To me travel is a triple delight: anticipation, performance, and _____. (Ilka Chase)

3. Science in general can be considered a technique with which fallible men try to outwit their own human propensities to fear the truth, to avoid it, to _____ it. (Abraham Maslow)

4. All the things I really like to do are either immoral, illegal, or _____. (Alexander Woollcott)

5. The only sensible ends of literature are, first, the pleasurable toil of writing; second, the gratification of one's family and friends; and, lastly, the solid _____. (Nathaniel Hawthorne)

6. Kindness in words creates confidence. Kindness in thinking creates profoundness. Kindness in giving creates _____. (Lao Tzu)

7. To speak logically, prudently, and _____ is a talent few possess. (Michel de Montaigne)

CONCLUSIONS

THREE WAYS TO FINISH

Free at last. Free at last. Thank God almighty we are free at last. (Martin Luther King, Jr.'s "I Have a Dream" speech)

The mystic chords of memory, stretching from every battlefield and patriot grave to every living hearth and hearthstone all over this broad land, will yet swell the chorus of the Union when again touched, as surely they will be, by the better angels of our nature. (Abraham Lincoln's first inaugural address)

I know not what course others may take; but as for me, give me liberty or give me death! (Patrick Henry before the Virginia Convention)

Each of the quotes above is from a famous speech. The lines are also the *concluding* lines of each speech.

Memory experts say that the human brain is most likely to retain the last thing it hears or reads. Therefore, whether you are writing a speech or an essay, it is important to finish strong. In the quotes above, the speakers wanted to leave their audiences with words that echo in the memory, words that smoothly bring their speeches to a close, and words that clearly and concisely sum up their main points.

Finding the perfect words to wrap up your essay can be challenging, but the following strategies will help.

1. **USE SIGNAL WORDS.** If you were driving on a highway that was coming to an end, you would hope for a road sign letting you know. The same is true with an essay. It's a good idea to give your reader a sign that you are about to wrap things up. Signal words like *in conclusion, finally, last,* and *in closing* are good road signs to let your reader know that you are about to finish.

2. **REPHRASE YOUR THESIS.** The key word here is *rephrase*. Don't just repeat or restate your thesis; instead, say it in a different way.

   EXAMPLE:
   Original Thesis: *Every child should have a pet because pets provide companionship, teach compassion, and encourage responsibility.*

   Rephrased Thesis: *Companionship, compassion, and responsibility are three things that we can give to our children in the form of a warm, cuddly, and furry friend.*

3. **COME FULL CIRCLE.** One excellent way to bring your essay to a smooth finish is to end where you began. Look back at the hook you used to introduce your essay and give some thought to how you might tie the end of your essay to the beginning. For example, if you began with an anecdote, you might refer to that anecdote again in the conclusion. This gives the reader the satisfying feeling of having come full circle.

Read the paragraphs below, which are the introduction and the conclusion to an essay about the benefits of the game of chess. Notice how the conclusion is tied to the introduction so that it brings the reader full circle.

INTRODUCTION

You are in control. You are the leader, and the success or failure of your realm depends on your ability to think, adapt, plan ahead, and execute. Are you an international diplomat, the CEO of a major corporation, or a field general leading troops into battle? You may be someday, but right now you are a child playing a game of chess. Chess has proven benefits for young people. It exercises their brains, improves their academic performance, and teaches them positive social skills.

CONCLUSION

Lastly, though some parents think it is the computer that is the key to preparing their children for the rigors of the 21st century, others turn to chess and its promise of increased brain power, increased success in school, and increased social skills. These parents know that the ancient game of kings and queens might just help their child someday become a success—perhaps even as a future diplomat, a CEO, or field general.

DO IT NOW Below is the introductory paragraph of an essay on public speaking. Read the paragraph and then write a concluding paragraph. Be sure to use signal words, rephrase the thesis, and bring the reader full circle.

Believe it or not, when people list their fears, the fear of giving a speech is often higher on the list than fear of death. You don't need to fear the podium more than the Grim Reaper. Three simple strategies will help you gain so much confidence that you might even look forward to public speaking. There are three keys to a successful speech: one, analyze your audience carefully; two, organize your ideas persuasively; and three, practice your words repeatedly.

COMPOUND WORD TRIADS

For the three words listed in each group below, find a single word that could be added to all three in order to form three new words or expressions. For example, *paper* can be added to all three words in the first item, to form the words *newspaper, sandpaper,* and *flypaper.*

THREE WORDS	WORD IN COMMON	THREE NEW WORDS
1. news, sand, fly	*paper*	*newspaper, sandpaper, flypaper*
2. skin, Latin, iron		
3. storage, turkey, feet		
4. scape, walk, beam		
5. mail, board, eye		
6. under, watch, top		
7. light, stand, hunter		
8. love, business, chain		
9. burn, transplant, ache		
10. hide, boy, bell		
11. aid, stand, wagon		
12. spot, alley, date		
13. out, elephant, sauce		
14. span, boat, jacket		
15. chime, surf, sock		

Now try to come up with at least three compound triads of your own. If you are having trouble thinking of any, use a dictionary.

EXTRAS

TIMED WRITING

DIVIDE YOUR TIME INTO THREE PHASES

More than ever before, students today often face the challenge of writing an essay under timed conditions. For example, you may be required to write an essay for your English class, for a state mandated test, or for the new SAT. All these tests require you to write within the constraints of a time limit, so learning how to produce good writing under time pressures is important.

The good news is that you can use the power of *three* to help you craft an excellent essay, whether you have a week or only 20 minutes to write. The most important thing to remember is the basic rule of three: When faced with a writing task, think of *three* things to say on the topic.

Begin by reading the directions carefully and by making sure you know how much time you will have. Then divide your time into three phases: planning, writing, and revising.

PHASE 1—PLANNING:

Spend no less than 10% of your time planning your essay. First, read the question carefully at least twice. Then do a quick brainstorm and generate a three-pronged thesis, which will serve as your rough outline. For each of the three prongs, jot down ideas you might use for evidence. Remember the three kinds of evidence: examples, facts, and quotes. If you spend time planning, you have a better chance of writing an essay that is clear, persuasive, and well organized.

PHASE 2—WRITING:

The bulk of your time—probably 70-80%—should be spent writing. If you have done an effective job of planning your essay, the task of writing will be much easier. With a clear thesis, you will have a rough outline. You will have a direction for your writing and will be less likely to run into roadblocks or detours. Likewise, you will be much more likely to write an essay that is easy for your reader to follow.

Begin with a hook in your introduction, followed by your thesis. Continue with the paragraphs in the body of your paper, and finish with a conclusion that brings your essay to a smooth ending.

PHASE 3—REVISING:

Spend no more than 10% of your time revising your essay. In most cases you will not have time to write a rough draft under timed writing conditions, so it makes sense to spend most of your time in planning and writing a solid first draft. Remember that you are not expected to write a perfect essay under timed writing conditions. Simply read over your draft, looking for any glaring errors in spelling, grammar, or mechanics. If you have written a clear thesis and followed through in the body of your paper, even a first draft will be clear, coherent, and persuasive enough to impress your reader.

With a clear writing strategy, you will not waste any precious time, and you'll stay calm, cool, and collected. You may still have some nervous energy, but that is not necessarily a bad thing. Instead of allowing the nervous energy to turn to panic, you will be able to channel the energy in a positive direction.

TIMED WRITING PRACTICE

Spend at least 10% of your time planning, 70-80% your time writing,
and no more than 10% revising.

DO IT NOW Consider carefully the statements below:

The very essence of leadership is that you have to have vision. You can't blow an uncertain trumpet.
—Theodore M. Hesburgh

Leadership is the art of getting someone else to do something you want done because he wants to do it.
—Dwight Eisenhower

Effective leadership is not about making speeches or being liked; leadership is defined by results, not attributes.
—Peter Drucker

What are the qualities that make a leader either effective or ineffective? In an essay, support your position by discussing evidence from your reading, your experience, or your observation. Use the Essay Planning Sheet on the next page to sketch out your ideas before you write.

ESSAY PLANNING SHEET

QUESTION:

_____

_____

THESIS

TOPIC SENTENCE	TOPIC SENTENCE	TOPIC SENTENCE

EVIDENCE	EVIDENCE	EVIDENCE

ABBREVIATIONS FOR EVIDENCE: E = EXAMPLES, F/S = FACT/STATISTICS, Q = QUOTES

TIMED ESSAY
AN EXAMPLE

Consider carefully the quotations below. What is the relationship between failure and success? Is an understanding of failure really important in achieving ultimate success?

In an essay, support your position by discussing evidence from your reading, your experience, or your observation.

Failure is the foundation of success, and the means by which it is achieved.
—Lao Tzu

If you're not failing every now and again it's a sign that you're not trying anything very innovative.
—Woody Allen

A man's errors are his portals of discovery.
—James Joyce

FAILURE: SPRINGBOARD TO SUCCESS

Two students, John and Mary, receive their math quizzes back from their teacher. John earns an A, answering every problem correctly. Mary earns a C, with several incorrect answers. Is it possible that in the long run Mary will learn more from her errors than John will from his correct answers? In many cases the answer is *yes*, because—under the right conditions—failure can be a useful stepping-stone to success. The proof of this paradoxical claim can be found in the examples of our great explorers, leaders, and business innovators.

Failure has been an important teacher for some of our great explorers. For example, today we think of Christopher Columbus as a successful explorer, but in his own time he failed miserably in his goal of finding a new route to the East. His three voyages west failed to deliver either gold or spices; as a result, he was stripped of most of his honors, put in chains, and branded a disgrace by his contemporaries. In the end, however, history has redeemed Columbus. His intrepid spirit of adventure changed history. Even though he failed to find a shipping lane to Asia, he succeeded in finding a new world. Another explorer schooled by failure was Ernest Shakelton. When he failed to become the first man to reach the South Pole, he modified his goals and set out to lead the first expedition to cross Antarctica. When his ship was caught in drifting ice, he realized that he had once again failed. Instead of giving up, he modified his goals once more and resolved to bring every man on the expedition home safely. He then pressed on, without his ship, to travel by small boat over 1000 miles and another 150 miles on foot in some of the most unforgiving conditions imaginable. Facing driving storms, glacial mountains, and arctic cold, he overcame unbelievable odds to succeed, delivering his entire crew safely. These explorers show us that time and attitude can turn failure into success.

CONTINUED

Great leaders have also learned lessons from failure. In May 1940 at Dunkirk, 335,000 Allied soldiers barely escaped capture by the German Army. It was an embarrassing retreat and a crushing defeat, but the Allies refused to give in to failure. Winston Churchill, the English prime minister, inspired the British people with his powerful words and his stubborn refusal to give up. The Allies rebounded to win victory in World War II. Today, instead of a defeat, the retreat at Dunkirk is seen as a symbol of the power of the human spirit to triumph in the face of the most dire and dark circumstances. Another example of a leader schooled by failure is Abraham Lincoln. Overcoming several lost elections and other failures in his early career, including losing a Senate election that followed his famous debate with Stephen Douglas, Lincoln rebounded from his failures to be elected president in 1860. But at the height of his greatest personal victory came the Civil War that threatened to destroy the nation he led. Despite this setback, Lincoln pressed forward, striving and persevering for five long, bloody years in the struggle to keep the young nation together. Churchill and Lincoln teach us that good leaders have the ability to refuse defeat and to transform failure into success.

Failure has been a tutor for business innovators as well as for explorers and politicians. Many view Thomas Edison as the greatest single inventor in history. Edison himself, however, always kept a much more careful tally of his failures than his successes. In his mind, each of his thousands of failures in the laboratory was not a defeat but instead an opportunity to learn something new. A more modern example of failure breeding success is the Post-It Note. When a 3M Corporation scientist came up with a glue that didn't stick, no one except its inventor saw anything but failure. The scientist, Spencer Silver, kept searching for an application for his adhesive. It wasn't until years later that another 3M employee came up with the idea that turned Silver's "failure" into a worldwide office supply success story. Business innovators show that with the proper attitude and effort, today's failures can be turned into tomorrow's successes.

To conclude, the lessons of failure have been successfully studied and applied by explorers, leaders, and business innovators. But what about those two math students we started with? Well, John, who received an A on the quiz, became a bit complacent with his success; as a result, he did not go over his notes and quizzes in preparation for the final exam. In contrast, Mary carefully reviewed every mistake she made on each quiz. In the end, John earned a C on the final exam and a B in the class. Mary, however, earned an A on the final and a B+ for the class. Thus, whether you are an explorer, world leader, business person, or student, you have a choice. You can either allow failure to defeat you, or you can use it as a springboard to ultimate success.

THIRTY-THREE TERRIFIC TOPICS

Writing is one third imagination, one third experience,
and one third observation. —William Faulkner

DO IT NOW Here are some writing ideas. Select one of the topics and do some brainstorming. Then write a thesis using your three best ideas.

1. Three stories every child should learn.
2. Three ways to beat procrastination.
3. Three reasons children should have pets.
4. Three causes of poor grades.
5. Three keys to good conversation.
6. Three ways that teens can resolve conflicts with their parents.
7. The three worst days of the week.
8. Three worst household chores.
9. Three ways to efficiently keep your room clean.
10. Three things to do when you are accepting an award.
11. Three things to do when you talk to the press.
12. Three strategies for winning your favorite game.
13. Three things that make an annual event memorable and worth attending.
14. Three creative alternative uses for a paper clip.
15. Three three-word slogans/sentences you might put on a T-shirt.
16. Three products you would be happy to sell.
17. Three people you know who have influenced you.
18. Three most fearful common human experiences and how to deal with them.
19. Three most frustrating human experiences and how to deal with them.
20. Three ways to be kind.
21. Three things you can do when life looks like it is not worth living.
22. Three books that everyone should read.
23. Three ways to manage procrastination.
24. Three ways to keep cool in an emergency situation.
25. Three songs that would be on the soundtrack of your life story.
26. Three reasons to stay in school.
27. Three ways to succeed in school.
28. Three reasons you always buy a specific product.
29. Three people you would induct into your personal hall of fame.
30. Three things everyone should learn to do.
31. Three traits of a good teacher.
32. Three common mistakes to avoid when planning a party.
33. Three guidelines for time management.

THREE TERRIFIC TOPICS

DO IT NOW Come up with three possible essay topics of your own. Use the list of key words below to get you thinking.

three examples	*three facts*	*three types*
three differences	*three mistakes*	*three steps*
three causes	*three places*	*three effects*
three reasons	*three guidelines*	*three traits*
three similarities	*three criteria*	*three parts*
three people	*three characteristics*	*three actions*

Topic #1: _____

_____

_____

Topic #2: _____

_____

_____

Topic #3: _____

_____

_____

Power of Three
Guidelines at a Glance

GENERAL RULE:
When faced with a writing task, think of three things you can say about your topic.

FOR BRAINSTORMING:
Brainstorm many ideas; then, pick your three best.

FOR WRITING A THESIS:
A good thesis statement has three "p's." It is a three-pronged parallel preview of your paper.

FOR ORGANIZING AN ESSAY:
Use the three ideas from your thesis as the basis for each of the topic sentences
in the three body paragraphs of your essay.

FOR SUPPORTING A THESIS:
Include three key types of evidence to support your topic sentences:
examples, facts, and quotations.

FOR WRITING INTRODUCTIONS:
Use one of these three hooks to grab the reader's interest:
conflict, mystery, metaphor.
or
one of these three:
anecdote, startling fact or statistic, quotation
or
one of these three:
hyperbole, bizarre image, countering conventional wisdom.

FOR WRITING FLUENT SENTENCES:
Use three techniques to write fluent sentences:
varied sentence openings, varied sentence length, and parallelism.

FOR WRITING CONCLUSIONS:
Use signal words, rephrase the thesis, and come full circle.

FOR TIMED WRITING:
Divide your time into three phases: planning, writing, and revision.

Essay
Example #1

A MIRACLE CURE-ALL

It makes you healthier, reduces stress and depression, and increases the quality of your sleep. It also reduces traffic and pollution, saves you money, and conserves energy. What is this miracle cure-all? Is it some kind of new discovery or some kind of amazing new fitness product? It's none of these; in fact, it is something that has been around as long as people have been putting one foot in front of another. It is walking. With so many potential positives, it's time to take a new look at this very old practice. The health benefits, psychological benefits, and financial benefits of walking make it possibly the best modern alternative for getting from point A to point B.

The health benefits are so numerous that you might be compelled to go out for a walk even before you finish this essay. For example, a walking program reduces the likelihood of heart disease, diabetes, osteoporosis, arthritis, and cancer. A study by the Harvard School of Public Health shows that walking reduces the risk of stroke by 40% (Gorman 36). With so many positives, one would think that beginning a walking program would be difficult—not so. Walking is the most natural, safe, and cheap form of preventative medicine there is. Dr. Joann Manson, chief of preventative medicine at Harvard's Brigham and Woman's Hospital says, "If everyone in the U.S. were to walk briskly 30 minutes a day, we could cut the incidence of many chronic diseases 30% to 40% (Gorman 36). Cutting disease and promoting good health are just the beginning of a long list of positives.

In addition to benefiting the body, walking also benefits the mind. For example, according to Mark Fenton, editor of the Boston-based *Walking Magazine*, the benefits of walking are immense: "We see again and again that regular exercise gives an improved sense of self-worth and an improved sense of purpose…It's also clear that regular activity may reduce the likelihood of clinical depression…" (Walking as a Way of Life). One study showed that depressed patients who exchanged their antidepressants for a walking program were less likely to relapse than those patients who took antidepressants (Gorman 38). As America's population grows older, walking increases the probability that an aging population can take care of itself and remain active and independent. Walking also increases an individual's sense of place and community. For example, when people are out walking, they learn the lay of the land and talk to neighbors they never would have encountered driving their cars. These psychological benefits alone make a stroll through the neighborhood a smart choice.

The final and least obvious benefit of walking is financial savings. Certainly the health and psychological benefits translate to money saved, but walking also reduces the cost of transportation. A national personal transportation survey found that 40% of all car trips are less than two miles in length. Replacing short car trips with walking could save gas money and reduce

CONTINUED

roadway congestion and pollution (Benefits of Walking). In fact, one international automobile company, KIA, is promoting what it calls the "Walking Bus," where a group of children, supervised by adults, walk from home to school together instead of taking a bus (Walking Bus). If a car company can see the financial advantage of fewer cars on the road, certainly private citizens should see the wisdom of walking over driving.

In conclusion, the many benefits of walking are almost too numerous to believe. How could one activity promise so many benefits for the body, the mind, and the pocketbook? If you are still not convinced, try it yourself. Get up right now, and walk.

WORKS CITED:

"Benefits of Walking: Transportation Benefits." Pedestrian and Bicycle Information Center. 6 May 2005. walkinginfo.org/pp/benefits/qualben/index.htm.

Gorman, Christine. "Walk, Don't Run." *Time Magazine*. 21 Jan. 2002: 36-38.

"Walking as a Way of Life." 27 April 2005. U.S. Department of Transportation, Federal Highway Administration. 5 May 2005. tfhrc.gov/safety/pedbike/articleswayolife.htm.

"Walking Bus." KIA Motors. 5 May 2005. walkingbus.org/whylife.html.

Essay
Example #2

WHY MEMORIZE AND RECITE?

RICHARD CORY

Whenever Richard Cory went down town,
We people on the pavement looked at him:
He was a gentleman from sole to crown
Clean favored, and imperially slim.

And he was always quietly arrayed,
And he was always human when he talked;
But still he fluttered pulses when he said,
"Good morning," and he glittered when he walked.

And he was rich – yes, richer than a king —
And admirably schooled in every grace:
In fine we thought that he was everything
To make us wish that we were in his place.

So on we worked, and waited for the light,
And went without the meat, and cursed the bread:
And Richard Cory, one calm summer night,
Went home and put a bullet through his head.

—Edwin Arlington Robinson

Being required to memorize and recite a passage or poem, such as the one above, is a pre-posterous idea. At least this is what Forrest Hainline, a successful attorney, thought as a college student when his poetry professor assigned poems for memorization. When he confronted his professor and demanded a justification, his professor responded: "Forrest, in twenty, thirty, or forty years, would you rather have made a few poems a part of your soul, part of the warp and woof of your being? Or would you rather not remember, and not have any need or desire to remember, the interpretation you gave to a poem no lines of which you can recall?" Forrest responded by devouring all the poems, reading them over and over until they became as familiar as his own name. As a result, he not only aced his final exam, he also gained a lifetime memory anthology of the greatest writing in the English language (Gleb 194). The act of memorizing and reciting passages of prose and poetry has multiple benefits, including improved reading, improved writing, and improved presentation skills.

First, memorizing and reciting improves reading by building vocabulary, by making the reader active rather than passive, and by establishing positive reading habits. Learning a passage by heart forces the reader to interact with the text. It's impossible to be a passive reader when reading and re-reading a passage in preparation for reciting it. When a student memorizes a passage or poem, he is likely to encounter a wide range of descriptive vocabulary, and the process of memorizing vocabulary in its proper context increases the likelihood that a student will be able to draw a word and its correct meaning from long-term memory. For example, a student reading Edwin Arlington Robinson's "Richard Cory" would encounter a description of Cory: "And he was always quietly arrayed." The one-time reader would probably not catch the nuance of the word "quietly" used to describe a person's dress, but through repetition, the reader who memorizes the passages would come to realize the unique use of the word to capture Cory's combination of humility and class. The poet Donald Hall argues that reading aloud and reciting are vital components for building fluent readers:

> If when we read silently we do not hear a text, we slide past words passively, without making decisions, without knowing or caring…We might as well be watching haircuts or "Conan the Barbarian." In the old Out-Loud Culture, print was always potential speech; even silent readers, too shy to read aloud, inwardly heard the sound of words. Their culture identified print and voice. Everyone's ability to read was enhanced by recitation. Then we read aggressively; then we demanded sense (Hall).

Passive reading makes for poor reading; the act of recitation and memorization makes the reader pay attention and encourages active reading.

In addition to improving reading, memorization and recitation also helps students polish their presentation and speaking skills. Standing in front of a group of people and reciting a passage from memory requires great poise and confidence. The student must recall the passage, but must also remain calm under pressure in order to communicate clearly to a real audience. A student who stands before a group and completes an effective recitation of a Shakespearean sonnet, for example, must spend hours practicing and polishing a presentation. In the process, the student learns how to memorize content and how to pass on that content to an audience. He witnesses firsthand how an audience can be awakened by a spirited interpretation or put to sleep by a half-hearted, uninspired effort. In doing this, a student learns the vital difference between "reading" a speech and "giving" a speech. When giving a speech, the presenter must interpret the words and express them in a manner that is appropriate to the tone of the passage and the connotations of the individual words. A student who at first mutters or mumbles when asked to read in class will learn to speak up and speak out. She will learn how to project her voice, how to control pitch and stress, and how to control and manipulate her voice to breathe life into the dead words on the page. Through memorization and recitation, the student "will discover drama, humor, passion and intelligence in print" (Hall). She will also develop her confidence, effectiveness, and poise in any public speaking situation.

Memorization and recitation not only make good speakers; they also build good writers. The process of reading and re-reading a passage helps a student to internalize the rhythm and syntax of the language. With either prose or poetry, the student is exposed to all the writer's weapons—such stylistic armory as imagery, figurative language, parallelism, and sentence variety. For example, a student memorizing Edwin Arlington Robinson's "Richard Cory" would be exposed to a master class in how to describe a character:

CONTINUED

> *He was a gentleman from sole to crown,*
> *Clean favored and imperially slim.*
>
> *And he was always quietly arrayed,*
> *And he was always human when he talked;*
> *But still he fluttered pulses when he said,*
> *"Good morning," and he glittered when he walked.*

Following Robinson's example, the young writer would see that you don't just tell the reader that your character is special; you show your reader with details like "fluttered pulses" and "glittered when he walked." By reading, hearing, and speaking them over and over again, a student begins to understand the variety of language patterns at a writer's disposal. By becoming intimate with the words of master writers, a student develops a repertoire of strategies to draw upon in his own writing. Great writers don't just pick up a pen and start writing classics; instead, they read, study, recite, and learn from their predecessors. For example, Shakespeare read and completed daily recitations from classical authors at his Stratford grammar school; a young Winston Churchill won a prize by reciting 1,200 lines of Macauley's *Days of Ancient Rome*; and the great English poet and lexicographer Samuel Johnson, when he had just learned to read, was required to memorize passages from the *Book of Common Prayer* (Turner D4). Learning by rote may not seem like a very creative activity, but it fires the embers of a young writer's imagination and opens the mind to the limitless possibilities of putting pen to paper.

Memorizing and reciting prose and poetry makes for more literate readers, imaginative writers, and articulate speakers. Imagine two students writing an in-class essay on the question, "Does the outward appearance of a person reflect the person's true character?" Student One has no experience memorizing or reciting; he just writes the routine essay, using clichés like "Don't judge a book by its cover." In contrast, Student Two has a memory anthology to draw upon, developed through memorization and recitation. She can go beyond the clichés and draw upon themes and images from literature and history; she can do more than name-drop because, through memorization, she has read, understood, and internalized some of the great works of the past and some of the universal themes of prose and poetry. She remembers Richard Cory, the millionaire that everyone admired, but who shot himself "one calm summer night." The student begins her essay: "He was a gentleman from sole to crown, clean favored and…"

WORKS CITED

Gleb, Michael J. *Discover Your Genius: How to Think Like History's Ten Most Revolutionary Minds.* New York: HarperCollins, 2003.

Hall, Donald. "Bring Back the Out-Loud Culture." *Newsweek* 15 April 1985: 12.

Turner, Dale. "Committing Psalms, Poems to Memory Yields Incorruptible Treasure." *Seattle Times* 11 Mar. 1995: D4.

Thinking in Threes © Taylor & Francis

Permission is granted to photocopy or reproduce this page for single classroom use only.

97

ANSWER KEYS

ANSWER KEYS

THREE, THREE, THREE, PAGE 11
Answers will vary. Possibilities:
1. There are *three* strikes in baseball.
2. In stories, a genie always grants *three* wishes.
3. There's a saying, "The *third* time's the charm."

TRIPLETS, PAGE 12
On the second part, answers will vary. Some possibilities:

1. dinner
2. Rock
3. fork
4. bears
5. see no evil
6. Ready
7. stock
8. happiness
9. Judicial
10. crackle
11. tomorrow
12. Animal
13. skip
14. blue
15. Win

1. Stop, look, and listen.
2. Morning, noon, and night.
3. Planes, trains, and automobiles.
4. The good, the bad, and the ugly.
5. Going, going, gone.
6. Me, myself, and I.

THREE THINGS TO SAY, PAGE 13
Answers will vary. Possibilities:
1. What are three characteristics that make you unique?
2. What are three things about your hometown that might be used to promote tourism?
3. What are three things you like about *American Idol*?
4. What are three things a person should *not* do during a speech?
5. What are three reasons why children should have pets?
6. What are three ways to be kind on a daily basis?
7. What are three qualities of an effective leader?
8. What are three things you like about *Harry Potter and the Prisoner of Azkaban*?

JUST THREE WORDS, PAGE 14
Answers will vary. Possibilities:
1. Three most important words in the English language: *I love you.*
2. The three best words for dealing with disappointment: *chocolate ice cream.*
3. Three most important words to remember for achieving success: *Follow your dream.*

BRAINSTORMING PRACTICE, PAGE 19
Answers will vary. Possibilities:
What are some ways to be kind on a daily basis?
1. Smile at people all the time.
2. Say "Thank you" and "You're welcome."
3. Have flowers delivered to all your teachers.
4. Send small gifts, anonymously.
5. Genuinely compliment others.
6. Buy candy for all your friends.
7. Tell friends and family how much you love them.
8. Do a favor for someone.
9. Never disagree with anyone.
10. Pick up your parents' dry cleaning for them.
11. Don't complain when your parents ask you to do something.
12. Adopt animals at the Humane Society.
13. Do someone a favor before they ask.
14. Let your little sister listen to her annoying music in your car on the way to school.
15. Agree to do all the chores at home.
16. Let your little brother play video games instead of making him stop so you can watch *American Idol.*
17. Buy your best friend lunch.
18. Don't complain about Brussels sprouts at dinner.
19. Pick up litter, even if it's not yours.
20. Don't say cruel things to others, even if you feel like it.

Three possible best ideas: Say "Thank you" and "You're welcome," genuinely compliment others, and do someone a favor before they ask.

ADVICE IN THREES, PAGE 20
1. *Knock* on wood.
2. *Live* and learn.
3. *Pay* the piper.
4. *Read* my lips.
5. *Break* a leg.
6. *Read* my mind.
7. *Take* the plunge.
8. *Cross* the line.
9. *Break* my heart.
10. *Hit* the roof.

Answers will vary on the next part. Possibilities:
1. Call your mother.
2. Seize the day.
3. Repeat after me.
4. Rise and shine.
5. Do your homework.
6. Take good notes.
7. Eat your vegetables.

8. Don't drive drunk.
9. Beware of dog.
10. Bury the hatchet.

PRACTICE WITH PARALLEL FORM, PAGE 25

Answers will vary. Possibilities:

1. Sports benefit your overall health because they relieve stress in your muscles, work your cardiovascular system, and supply your brain with oxygen.
2. Correct.
3. William Shakespeare is influential because of his poetry, his plays, and his talent for coining new words.
4. Every student should complete high school because high school graduates earn more, find better jobs, and have more choices.
5. Correct.

PRACTICE WRITING A THESIS, PAGE 26

Answers will vary. Possibility:

A good leader is someone who is charismatic, good at his or her job, and able to keep control.

PUTTING IT TOGETHER, PAGE 27

Answers will vary. Possibilities:

Question: How can you be kind on a daily basis?
Top three brainstormed answers: Say "Thank you" and "You're welcome," genuinely compliment others, and do someone a favor before they ask.
Thesis: People can be kind on a daily basis by saying "Thank you" and "You're welcome," by genuinely complimenting others, and by doing someone a favor before he or she asks.

THREE IMPORTANT THINGS, PAGE 28

Answers will vary. Possibilities:

1. The three most important things to remember about pimples are that they affect everyone, they go away eventually, and they aren't nearly as noticeable as you think they are.
2. The three keys to life are doing what you love, finding someone to love, and loving yourself.
3. Success in music requires three things: practice, patience, and more practice.

THREES IN ACTION, PAGE 34

Answers will vary. Possibilities:

Thesis Statement: Thomas Edison's genius was the perfect combination of innovative thinking, hard work, and a positive attitude.
Topic Sentence Paragraph #1: No one before or after Edison

has demonstrated such a capacity for innovative thinking.
Topic Sentence #2: In addition to his creative genius, Edison also had a legendary capacity for hard work.
Topic Sentence Paragraph #3: Even though the combination of creativity and tireless drive made Edison a success, perhaps his more noteworthy trait was his positive attitude.

Answers will vary. Possible answer:

The Perfect Combination

He was named the man of the millennium by *Life* magazine; he was *Parade Magazine*'s top American innovator; and he made it into the top 40 in a book that ranked the most influential persons of all time. Although he died in 1931, no one has come close to the creative energy and productivity of inventor Thomas Edison. His genius was the perfect combination of innovative thinking, hard work, and a positive attitude.

No one before or after Edison has demonstrated such a capacity for innovative thinking. Edison generated an amazing quantity of new ideas and transformed those ideas into practical inventions that changed the lives of every man, woman, and child in America. He held over one thousand patents. The light bulb, phonograph, motion picture camera, telegraph, telephone, and typewriter are just a few of the innovations he either developed or improved (Hart 223). Not only were his ideas numerous, they were also practical. Edison's innovative thinking laid the foundation for the modern research laboratory. His Menlo Park laboratory was the prototype for modern companies such as General Electric that bring teams of people together to research, test, and manufacture the latest technology (Maxwell 84). Certainly he did not do everything alone; instead, his creative energy allowed him to work with and motivate others to produce and implement his ideas.

In addition to his creative genius, Edison also had a legendary capacity for hard work. Even though it took over ten thousand tries to find the correct materials for the incandescent light bulb, he did not give up until he found the answer. Many inventors would be fulfilled after filing a patent for just one invention, but Edison drove himself tirelessly to create, test, and improve his inventions. According to Edison biographer Neil Baldwin, "He was proud of the fact that certain times of the year he was away from home for one hundred nights in a row working in the lab" (Lamb 144). For Edison there was no retirement; only his death, in 1931 at age 84, put an end to his work.

Even though the combination of creativity and tireless drive made Edison a success, perhaps his more noteworthy trait was his positive attitude. Although he had only four months of formal education and was labeled "retarded" by one of his school teachers,

CONTINUED

Edison pursued his own education and achieved so much that today his name is synonymous with genius (Hart 222). Later in life he suffered from deafness, but did not let this obstacle stop him. Instead, he went on to fill countless homes with music through the invention of the phonograph. When his laboratory burned down in 1914, he immediately rebuilt it and continued to work for another seventeen years. There was no "quit" in the man who said, "If we did all the things we were capable of doing, we would literally astound ourselves" (Maxwell 89).

The life of Thomas Alva Edison was clearly astounding. His innovative thinking, his hard work, and his positive attitude allowed him to reach the apex of human potential. In Edison, the three chords of inspiration, perspiration, and attitude combined to create a symphony of achievements that should be a reminder to each of us that the only limits that exist in this world are the limits that we create in our own minds.

THREE-PEAT AFTER ME, PAGE 37

Answers will vary. Possibilities:
1. Sales, sales, sales.
2. Scandal, scandal, scandal.
3. Love, love, love.
4. Honesty, honesty, honesty.
5. Practice, practice, practice.
6. Courage, courage, courage.
7. Army, army, army.

The original quotes:
1. Three things make you a winner in this business: timing, timing. And, of course, timing. (Harry Benson)
2. There are three things which the public will always clamor for, sooner or later: namely, novelty, novelty, and novelty. (Thomas Hood)
3. The world rests on three things: money, money, and money.
4. Patience, patience, patience! The first, and last, and the middle virtue of a politician. (John Adams)
5. Dancing is just discovery, discovery, discovery. (Martha Graham)
6. To succeed as a conjurer, three things are essential—first, dexterity; second, dexterity; and third, dexterity.
7. To go to war three things must be ready: money, money, and once again money. (Gian Giacomo Di Trivulzio)

Write your own three-peat sentence: The key to playing ragtime piano is syncopation, syncopation, syncopation.

USE THREE TYPES OF EVIDENCE, PAGES 41-42

Answers will vary. Possibility:

Bowling is a great recreational activity because it encourages physical fitness. For those who are discouraged by intense physical activity, bowling offers a way to get some exercise without even realizing it. In fact, statistics show that those who participate in a physical activity they enjoy are 80% more likely to do the activity on a regular basis. In addition, Lester Strikesalot, president of the International Bowling League, says, "People who do sporting activities with others, such as bowling, are ten times more likely to participate in physical exercise."

EXAMPLES NEED THREE QUALITIES, PAGE 43

Relevant examples:
1. He made up over 1,700 new words.
2. His words and phrases are quoted in written and spoken English more than any other single writer's.

Item that is not specific:
1. Because there has been such an amazing growth in entertainment options over the past ten years, young people choose to sit in front of their computer or their television rather than read a newspaper.

Most varied outline:
Outline #1. It includes an example from literature, an example from U.S. history, an example from the author's personal life.

PRACTICE WITH QUOTATIONS, PAGE 47

1. SQ: "[He] is living proof that if you work hard you can achieve almost anything."

2. IQ: Mike Lopresti, sportswriter for the USA Today, says that the most amazing statistic that shows Gwynn's amazing hitting is the fact that he struck out twice in a single game only 32 times in his 20-year professional baseball career.

3. DQ: U.S. Congresswoman Susan A. Davis praises Tony saying, "[He] is living proof that if you work hard you can achieve almost anything."

4. LQ: Experienced animal trainers take a stool with them when they step into a cage with a lion. Why a stool? It tames a lion better than anything—except maybe a tranquilizer gun. When the trainer holds the stool with the legs extended toward the lion's face, the animal tries to focus on all four legs at once. And that paralyzes him. Divided focus always works against you.

HALL OF FAME, PAGE 48
Answers will vary. The activity includes an example.

CALLING THE GAME, PAGE 51
Topic sentence: When it comes to efficiency of communication, e-mail has several advantages over the telephone.
One example of "play by play": Another factor that makes e-mail efficient is the fact that it creates a paper trail.
One example of "color commentary": Because e-mail records the times and dates of communication and the exact words that were exchanged, it is an easy and efficient way to create a communication archive.

WORN OUT WORDS, PAGE 53
1. under the gun
2. jump for joy
3. hit the hay
4. over the hill
5. mind over matter
6. jump the gun
7. feast or famine
8. out to lunch
9. make ends meet
10. bury the hatchet.

1. *With a cliché:* She knew she was under the gun to finish her project for the science fair.
Without a cliché: Under so much pressure to finish her project for the science fair, she felt as if she were being squeezed between two enormous slabs of concrete.
2. *With a cliché:* Tula couldn't help but jump for joy when her lost dog returned home.
Without a cliché: When her lost dog returned home, Tula felt as if every molecule in her body was rejoicing.
3. *With a cliché:* Ted decided to hit the hay after competing in the extreme eating challenge.
Without a cliché: After competing in the extreme eating challenge, Ted collapsed into bed, feeling as though all the hot dogs he ate were weighing down on top of him.
4. *With a cliché:* Mrs. Johnson complained that she was over the hill.
Without a cliché: Mrs. Johnson complained that she was looking a little too much like a grandmother.
5. *With a cliché:* He knew that beating the championship wrestler was a case of mind over matter.
Without a cliché: He knew that to beat the championship wrestler he had to picture his own muscles turning into solid steel.

6. *With a cliché:* Rebecca knew it was wrong to jump the gun and start eating dinner before the minister said grace, but she couldn't resist.
Without a cliché: Rebecca knew it was wrong to start eating before the minister had said grace, but the mashed potatoes and gravy hypnotized her and she scooped up a mound anyway.
7. *With a cliché:* In the restaurant business, it's either feast or famine.
Without a cliché: In the restaurant business, people crawl over each other to be seated on some days. Other days, the dining room is so bare that waiters and waitresses sit around, looking bored.
8. *With a cliché:* Fred was supposed to be watching the security camera, but it was obvious he was out to lunch.
Without a cliché: Fred was supposed to be watching the security camera, but his eyes were glazed over and registering nothing.
9. *With a cliché:* Priscilla found it hard to make ends meet in the big city.
Without a cliché: Priscilla could never make her pay check stretch to cover all her expenses in the big city.
10. *With a cliché:* He knew it was time to forgive his friend and bury the hatchet.
Without a cliché: He knew it was time to forgive his friend and lock up the strange monster of jealousy.

THREE WAYS TO "HOOK" THE READER, PAGE 57
1. A.
2. B
3. A.
4. B.

BEGINNING WITH CONFLICT, PAGE 59
Answers will vary. The activity includes examples.

BEGINNING WITH MYSTERY, PAGE 60
Answers will vary. The activity includes examples.

BEGINNING WITH METAPHOR, PAGE 61-62
Answers will vary. The activity includes examples.

THREE MORE WAYS TO "HOOK" THE READER, PAGE 63
Answers will vary. The activity includes examples.

CONTINUED

YET THREE MORE WAYS TO "HOOK" THE READER, PAGE 64

Answers will vary. The activity includes examples.

QUOTES WITH THREE, PAGE 65

Answers will vary. Possibilities:

1. love
2. entertaining
3. engineering
4. humility
5. adapt to old age
6. learn from our mistakes
7. pocketbooks
8. acceptance

The original quotes:

1. There are three classes of people: lovers of wisdom, lovers of humor, and lovers of gain. (Plato)
2. My father gave me three hints in public speaking: be sincere, be brief, and be seated. (James Roosevelt)
3. The three basic definitions of science:
If it's green or wiggles, it's biology.
If it stinks, it's chemistry.
If it doesn't work, it's physics. (Timothy J. Rolfe)
4. In every negotiation, three crucial elements are always present—information, time, and power.
5. There are three periods in life: youth, middle age, and "how well you look." (Nelson Rockefeller)
6. There exist only three beings worthy of respect: the priest, the soldier, the poet. To know, to kill, to create. (Charles Baudelaire)
7. Folks are serious about three things—their religion, their family, and, most of all, their money. (Bert Lance)
8. There are three parts in truth: first, the inquiry, which is the wooing of it; secondly, the knowledge of it, which is the presence of it; and thirdly, the belief, which is the enjoyment of it. (Francis Bacon)

THREE WAYS TO WRITE FLUENT SENTENCES, PAGE 69

Answers will vary. Possibility:

Paper clips are the most amazing office product ever invented. Paper clips are useful, easy to use, and fun. Unlike staples, you don't need a special device to attach them. There is no need to struggle to remove paper clips because these fantastic pieces of metal can be taken off with one easy motion. Paper clips can easily slip over a bundle of papers to keep them bound together firmly and neatly. Cheap entertainment can also be provided by paper clips. You can bend them into animal shapes, string them together into long chains, and you can even hold competitions. Each contestant receives five paper clips and the winner of the competition is the one who makes the most impressive sculpture. So you see, paper clips really are much more than simple malleable pieces of metal.

SENTENCE VARIETY, PAGE 70-71

Answers will vary. Possibilities:

1. Eager and restless, the students listened to the radio to find out whether or not school had been cancelled because of a snowstorm.
2. Loudly and clearly, Paul's mother told him to keep the toilet seat down.
3. Sitting in the living room, Mary thought about how to finish her project.
4. In his sweaty bowling shoes, Josh ran a record mile.
5. In order to improve his grades, Bill read an extra hour each night.
6. Because the teacher announced that the test was cancelled, the class cheered.

VARIETY IN SENTENCE LENGTHS, PAGE 72-73

Answers will vary. Possibilities:

1. Although Pedro spent all night on it, he was unable to finish the project.
2. Sheila spent three hours writing her essay, but she didn't spend any time proofreading it.
3. Our neighborhood ice-cream man is a big Elvis fan; therefore, his ice-cream truck plays a medley of Elvis tunes.

PARALLELISM, PAGE 74

Answers will vary. Possibilities:

1. I am the kind of person who loves to listen to music, shop for music, and play music.
2. Joe enjoys flossing before breakfast, flossing during lunch, and flossing after dinner.
3. Before I slipped in the shower and broke my leg, I ran a marathon, built a log home, and climbed Mount Everest.
4. Determined to improve my grades, I studied my notes, read my textbook, and wrote multiple drafts of my essays.
5. A good paper carrier needs to have three things: a strong back, a strong arm, and an accurate aim.

PARALLELISM IN ACTION, PAGE 76

Answers will vary. The originals:

1. Travel is fatal to prejudice, bigotry, and narrow-mindedness. (Mark Twain)
2. To me travel is a triple delight: anticipation, performance, and recollection. (Ilka Chase)
3. Science in general can be considered a technique with which fallible men try to outwit their own

human propensities to fear the truth, to avoid it, to distort it. (Abraham Maslow)

4. All the things I really like to do are either immoral, illegal, or fattening. (Alexander Woollcott)
5. The only sensible ends of literature are, first, the pleasurable toil of writing; second, the gratification of one's family and friends; and, lastly, the solid cash. (Nathaniel Hawthorne)
6. Kindness in words creates confidence. Kindness in thinking creates profoundness. Kindness in giving creates love. (Lao-Tse)
7. To speak logically, prudently, and adequately is a talent few possess. (Michel de Montaigne)

THREE WAYS TO FINISH, PAGE 79

In closing, though you may believe the Grim Reaper is out to get you when you step up to the podium, if you practice these three simple strategies, you need not fear a fate worse than death. You can feel confident that your speech will be a successful one and that with practice…who knows? You might even become an enthusiastic public speaker.

COMPOUND WORD TRIADS, PAGE 81

2. pig
3. cold
4. moon
5. black
6. dog
7. head
8. letter
9. heart
10. cow
11. band
12. blind
13. white
14. life
15. wind

Answers to the next part will vary. Possibilities:
Originals:
1. Cut, clip, jam. Add "paper" to get paper cut, paper clip, paper jam.
2. Note, store, mark. Add "book" to get notebook, bookstore, and bookmark.
3. Out, front, backer. Add "line" to get outline, front line, and linebacker.

TIMED WRITING PRACTICE, PAGE 86

Answers will vary. See "Timed Essay Example" on page 88 for sample.

THIRTY-THREE TERRIFIC TOPICS, PAGE 90

Answers will vary. Some possibilities:
Three of the worst household chores, all of which require a strong stomach, are cleaning the litter box, scrubbing the toilets, and cleaning out moldy containers at the back of the refrigerator.

THREE TERRIFIC TOPICS, PAGE 91

Answers will vary. Possibilities:
1. Three traits of an exceptional listener include focused attention on the speaker, use of listening cues (like nodding), and feedback to the speaker.
2. A person needs to follow these three steps to earn better grades: take notes, study for class, and get enough sleep.
3. Three places in the United States have proven to reduce stress and promote relaxation in its visitors: Sedona, Arizona; Carmel, California; and Taos, New Mexico.

About the Author

Brian Backman grew up in Seattle, Washington. After high school he served in the United States Army in Europe for three years. He then returned to Washington to attend Seattle Pacific University, where he earned a bachelor's degree in English and a master's in curriculum and instruction.

For the past fifteen years he has been on the faculty at Anacortes High School. He teaches English classes grades 9-12, including Advanced Placement English. He also coaches cross-country and is the faculty advisor for the Anacortes High School Key Club.

When not in the classroom, Backman enjoys strumming his guitar, playing basketball, and exploring the outdoors near his scenic home in Anacortes, Washington, a small town on Fidalgo Island, 85 miles northwest of Seattle. He also gains much inspiration from his wife, Joy, and two young sons, Sam and Max.

Common Core State Standards Alignment Sheet
Thinking in Threes

All lessons in this book align to the following standards.

Grade Level	Common Core State Standards
Grade 5 ELA-Literacy	W.5.2 Write informative/explanatory texts to examine a topic and convey ideas and information clearly. W.5.4 Produce clear and coherent writing in which the development and organization are appropriate to task, purpose, and audience. (Grade-specific expectations for writing types are defined in standards 1–3 above.) W.5.5 With guidance and support from peers and adults, develop and strengthen writing as needed by planning, revising, editing, rewriting, or trying a new approach. (Editing for conventions should demonstrate command of Language standards 1-3 up to and including grade 5 here.)
Grade 6 ELA-Literacy	W.6.2 Write informative/explanatory texts to examine a topic and convey ideas, concepts, and information through the selection, organization, and analysis of relevant content. W.6.4 Produce clear and coherent writing in which the development, organization, and style are appropriate to task, purpose, and audience. (Grade-specific expectations for writing types are defined in standards 1–3 above.) W.6.5 With some guidance and support from peers and adults, develop and strengthen writing as needed by planning, revising, editing, rewriting, or trying a new approach. (Editing for conventions should demonstrate command of Language standards 1–3 up to and including grade 6 here.)
Grade 7 ELA-Literacy	W.7.2 Write informative/explanatory texts to examine a topic and convey ideas, concepts, and information through the selection, organization, and analysis of relevant content. W.7.4 Produce clear and coherent writing in which the development, organization, and style are appropriate to task, purpose, and audience. (Grade-specific expectations for writing types are defined in standards 1–3 above.) W.7.5 With some guidance and support from peers and adults, develop and strengthen writing as needed by planning, revising, editing, rewriting, or trying a new approach, focusing on how well purpose and audience have been addressed. (Editing for conventions should demonstrate command of Language standards 1–3 up to and including grade 7 here.)
Grade 8 ELA-Literacy	W.8.2 Write informative/explanatory texts to examine a topic and convey ideas, concepts, and information through the selection, organization, and analysis of relevant content. W.8.4 Produce clear and coherent writing in which the development, organization, and style are appropriate to task, purpose, and audience. (Grade-specific expectations for writing types are defined in standards 1–3 above.) W.8.5 With some guidance and support from peers and adults, develop and strengthen writing as needed by planning, revising, editing, rewriting, or trying a new approach, focusing on how well purpose and audience have been addressed. (Editing for conventions should demonstrate command of Language standards 1–3 up to and including grade 8 here.)

Printed in the United States
by Baker & Taylor Publisher Services